SELF-HELP
FOR
SMARTIES

SELF-HELP
FOR
SMARTIES

Success Secrets for
Weight Loss,
Love and Sex,
Wealth
and Parenting

Irwin Gootnick, M.D.

𝒫ENMARIN BOOKS

ROSEVILLE, CALIFORNIA

Editorial Offices
Penmarin Books
1044 Magnolia Way
Roseville, CA 95661
(916) 771-5869

Sales and Customer Service Offices
Midpoint Trade Books
27 West 20th Street, Suite 1102
New York, NY 10011
(212) 727-0190

Penmarin Books are available at special discounts for bulk purchases for premiums, sales promotions, or education. For details, contact the publisher. On your letterhead, include information regarding the intended use of the book and how many you wish to purchase.

Visit our Web site at www.penmarin.com for more information about this and other exciting titles.

Author photo by Lisa Knutson.
Cover design by Mike Stromberg.

Printed in the United States of America
1 2 3 4 5 6 7 8 9 10   2010 2009 2008 2007 2006

ISBN 1-883955-41-6

Library of Congress Control Number: 2006901512

As a dear friend, mentor, original thinker, and creative teacher, he was a tremendous inspiration to me. He passed away in 2004, and I will continue to miss him, but his spirit lives on.

CONTENTS

Preface   ix

Introduction   xi

PART I

WHY YOU BEHAVE IN WAYS YOU HATE   **1**

Chapter 1   Guilt, Resentment, and the Self-
Destructive Behaviors They Cause   3

Chapter 2   Do You Think You're in Control of
Your Life?   15

Chapter 3   Guilt and Rebellion: Whose Life Is It
Anyway?   27

Chapter 4   Surviving Your Family   35

Chapter 5   Is Blaming Your Parents Justified?   55

Chapter 6   Charts: Looking at Yourself in the
Mirror and Seeing Your Family   69

PART II

**WHY IT'S HARD TO END YOUR SUFFERING
AND WHAT YOU CAN DO ABOUT IT**   **83**

Chapter 7   Your Family Was Flawed: Why You
Can't See the Damage   85

Chapter 8   Crime, Punishment, and Psychological
Jail   93

Chapter 9   Why Do You Feel Like a Victim?   97

Chapter 10   Assessing Yourself and Your Family
             Members   111

Chapter 11   Overcoming Accommodation, Rebellion,
             and Mimicking   129

Chapter 12   Double Trouble in Your Family   137

PART III

**SECRET SUCCESS CODES FOR
WEIGHT LOSS, LOVE AND SEX,
WEALTH, AND PARENTING**   **143**

Chapter 13   Why Am I Fat and Why Can't I Lose
             Weight?   145

Chapter 14   Why Can't I Fall in Love or Stay
             in Love?   169

Chapter 15   Why Do Success and Wealth
             Pass Me By?   197

Chapter 16   I've Become My Mother/Father and
             My Child Is a Pain   229

Afterword: Keeping the Hope Alive   261

Index   263

PREFACE

So many people are unhappy because they are trapped in repeated self-defeating behaviors with weight, love, career, and parenting, and are unable to change for the better no matter how much they desire to or try.

Isn't it remarkable that no matter how intelligent or well meaning the advice you get from magazines, books, experts, and friends, it is extremely difficult to successfully apply it to your life?

My purpose in writing *Self-Help for Smarties* was to help you change what you dislike in your life. I plan to show you what specifically happened to you to cause the behaviors you hate, to learn why it is so hard to change, and to provide you with simple and clear charts and real-life stories that will show you the way without psychobabble and complicated theories.

Acknowledgments

I would like to thank the following people for their valuable contributions.

Denise Pinhey helped me with the first editing, which involved the general layout of the book and the creation of titles for chapters, paragraphs, and real-life stories.

Nancy Greystone helped me to present my ideas in a more lively, easy-to-read, and stimulating style.

My friend Alison Segan suggested the title for the book.

My very dear friend, colleague, and original thinker, Dr. Joseph Weiss, who died this year, was inspirational for me. Some of the concepts in this book were influenced by his teachings. The special applications, charts, and self-help exercises are based on my thirty-seven years of clinical experience, teaching, and research.

—Irwin Gootnick
March 2006

INTRODUCTION

If you've tried to lose weight, but the scale never seems to change no matter how many diets you try, this book is for you. If each new relationship is as bad as the previous ones, this book is for you. If motivational speakers haven't motivated you, this book is for you. If you can't succeed with your career, and if your kids make you miserable despite a variety of parenting techniques, this book is for you. If the self-help books on your bedside table nearly outweigh self-help books on the shelves of the nearest bookstore and you *still* haven't been "helped," this book is for you.

Before we begin, I want you to remember these words: **Don't give up hope.** Though you may have tried to change lifelong patterns before and failed at your attempts, things *can* change, and when they do, your life *will* improve. It's as simple as that.

How many times in your life have you said or thought, "If I only had . . ."? "If I only had *said,* or if I only had *done* something differently"? As a psychiatrist I listen to people's stories of failure, regret, and frustration all the time. It's my job to ferret out what is behind the feelings of guilt and resentment that are so often expressed in my office, and then to help people change their self-defeating, lifelong patterns. It's my goal to help move them from a life of "If I only had . . ." to a life of "Aren't I lucky that I did."

People *do* want to change, but they often look in the wrong places to find the help to do so. What happens then is that they blame themselves for lacking willpower to find a way out of their misery.

If you feel you are one of these people, I repeat: **Don't give up hope.** This book is going to help you find the hidden reasons specific to you for your repeated failings and the depression and anxiety that so often go along with them. Once you're aware of these reasons, you'll finally be able to gain control of your life.

You won't have to decipher psychobabble, you won't have to decode complicated theories in order to learn what you need to know to change your life. You just have to read with a willingness to change.

Not Just Another Self-Help Book

Too often, even most well-intentioned self-help books fall short in their attempts to help you change. Why? Because while they do present general theories to describe what is responsible for people's problems, what they don't provide—and yet what you need—is information that's specific to your problems. Self-help books present lots of advice and many examples of people who have succeeded in overcoming their problems. What they leave out is an explanation of why it's so difficult for *you* to put their advice into practice and succeed for yourself. They neglect to explain why you keep repeating your self-defeating patterns.

And what about self-improvement seminars? They rarely delve into your hidden inhibitions—the ones you have no control over and yet that always block you from progressing beyond a certain point, and always leave you feeling frustrated. They too provide examples, but not the tools needed to recognize the *causes* of your specific problems. Since they rarely address how and why a particular family member's flaw negatively affected *your* life, all you can hope for is that some of the examples presented will—by coincidence—match some of your experience. If there's a match, you're in luck. If there isn't, you're still left in the dark as to how to make your life work better.

Led by speakers promising to teach you how to be more effective, more assertive, and more successful, self-help seminars don't take into account the hidden problems (or issues) that inhibit you from progressing into the realms the speakers assure you you'll reach. And so, just like the self-help books, these self-help seminars also leave you feeling frustrated.

Willpower and New Year's resolutions are two great ways we show our determination to change. Promises to God are another way we show our dedication to change: We'll be "good" if only He will help us solve our problems. But even if we *want* to change, *try* to change, and *pray* for help in making a change, sometimes we still fail. And then what?

I won't give you the usual lists you find in so many self-help books. You know the ones: "5 Ways to Instant Success," "10 Days to Lose 10 Unwanted Pounds," and on and on and on. Instead, I am going to help you see what is blocking you from following the advice. What I do give you is a solid understanding of your problems, where they came from, and how to use this information to change your behavior. It is my goal to give you the tools to help you uncover what *specifically happened to you* in your family—not general theories about unknown families.

You'll be able to see the problem relationships that you had with parents and/or siblings in a whole new way, and the profound negative effects they have had on your current life. With this newfound clarity you'll be able to rid yourself of your unwanted behavior patterns—patterns that make you unhappy and are often unhealthy.

This book will help you see what your family members have said and done that make you feel guilty, or rebellious, or even make you imitate the behaviors you hate in them. But most important, this book will help you understand why, despite knowing that your family was troubled, you never let yourself see how you were being negatively affected. Taking the huge (and courageous) step to begin to dig up long-buried information is critical to overcoming the behaviors that you want to change the most. I will guide you throughout your journey to growth and change.

You'll see how to finally *bust through deep guilt and resentment* that cause self-defeating behaviors. Whether these behaviors show up as failures in weight control, career achievement, love fulfillment, or parenting success, you can find the help needed to make lasting changes right here. This book is full of charts, self-assessment questions, and simple explanations of real-life examples. Use them and you'll be able to pinpoint problems your parents and siblings may have had, see how you were affected (negatively) by them, and then see how to use that information to change what you dislike about yourself

In this book, the negative family influences that have always been hidden from your conscious knowledge will be revealed. Applying this knowledge and understanding will lead you to success in overcoming the self-defeating behaviors that have held you back for so long.

Self-Help for Smarties offers concrete ways for you to gain quick access to understanding what's been holding you back. And once you see what this is, *Self-Help for Smarties* shows you *how* to make long-term changes in specific areas of your life.

What Goals Have You Sabotaged?

You'll see many here. Some might be pretty familiar to you. You'll understand that no matter how determined people are to overcome their self-defeating behaviors, change remains elusive to many of them.

What Diets Have You Tried and Why Are You Still Overweight?

How many times have you tried to lose weight? How much information on health, diet, and exercise have you read? Do you have any idea why you continue to fail and what keeps undermining your efforts? This book will help you see why you fail and then will show you how to use the information provided to overcome it and to start looking great and feeling great . . . about yourself.

What Disastrous Relationships Have You Entered into?

Are you constantly attracted to the bad apples while rejecting the good prospects? Do you run the other way when someone falls in love with you? Are you sexually hot in the beginning but become uninterested over time? Finding the right person and making it work *is* possible, but first you must discover which one of the six major underlying motivations causes you to repeatedly fail in your relationships. Once you've discovered it, you can clear the way for real love to enter.

What Financial or Career Plans Have You Damaged?

Frustrated? Demoralized? Wringing your hands while thinking "If only I had made that investment last year when I thought of it"? Do you sell when you should buy, buy instead of sell? Are you a perennial student hiding behind your textbooks, avoiding opportunities in the real world, passing up chances for success? If you *do* succeed, do you invariably then mess it up? I'll show you what accounts for this and how to change it.

What Do You Do to Alienate People?

Take a hard look at yourself. Are you self-centered, critical, or too authoritarian? Are you too passive? Do you feel sorry for people and give in to their every request until they have no respect for you? Do you resent authority, acting contrary, defiant, and stubborn with your superiors? Have you ever attended training seminars on sensitivity, assertiveness, leadership, setting goals, and so on, and did they honestly help? Reading the charts and examples you'll find here will shed light on your destructive old patterns while illuminating a path to healthy new ones.

What about Your Kids?

Are they a thorn in your side no matter what you try? Are you stuck in conflicts that don't get resolved regardless of the rewards or punishment you offer? Are you baffled about why your kids do poorly or have qualities you can't stand? Have you become like your own parents in spite of wanting to be different with your kids? There are reasons and solutions for these problems.

Self-Knowledge Is Power

The charts, self-assessment questions, explanations, and real-life examples from case histories in later chapters will enable you to quickly recognize the actual flaws of your parents and siblings, and the self-destructive ways that you have dealt with them in the past. Why is this knowledge so important? Because up until now all of these patterns have been hidden from your conscious mind, leaving you unable to do anything about them. But now you'll be able to identify the major parent or sibling flaw—authoritarian, weak, possessive, rejecting, competitive, perfectionistic, to name just a few—that's held you back. The charts you'll find here will help you see how your lifelong destructive behaviors were actually *responses* that you used to cope with the guilt and resentment you were feeling toward your flawed family members. Identifying and understanding where the behaviors started is the first step to making long-lasting life changes.

How to Use This Book

This book is for you, and only you will know how to make it work best for you. If you know you've bought this book for problems with love and want to jump ahead to that particular chapter, feel free to do it now. Jumping ahead, zeroing in on something specific to your own issues is definitely one way to use this book. However, if reading it chapter by chapter, cover to cover, is what works for you, go on and do it. It's up to you because it's *for* you.

There's another part of *Self-Help for Smarties* that is geared specifically for you. At the end of each chapter you'll find a feature called "Exercise: Now Look at Yourself." These exercises are designed to help you continue processing the information that you received in the chapter. Do you have to do them? Again, the answer is up to you; they're there if you want them, now or in the future.

Having said that, there is, of course, an exception to that rule. You'll find no exercises at the end of the chapters that contain charts. The reason? In those chapters, the charts themselves are the exercise, and so doing them throughout the chapter is enough. So get ready to set sail. Your voyage of self-discovery is about to launch.

PART I

WHY YOU BEHAVE

IN WAYS YOU

HATE

CHAPTER 1

Guilt, Resentment, and the Self-Destructive Behaviors They Cause

PEOPLE TELL ME OVER AND over how "impossible" it seems to change their unwanted attitudes and that they have "no idea" why this is. If you're reading this book, clearly you want to make changes in your life. If you want these changes to last, you'll need to understand the how and why of guilt and resentment. *How* things you experienced in dealing with your parents and siblings created self-defeating patterns in you. *Why* these very same self-defeating patterns keep you from functioning as well as you can, or from being the person you'd like to be. All the willpower you have and the new year's resolutions you make will not help you function better or assist you in becoming the person you truly do want to be. Why? Because long after you've left your family, your childhood patterns continue to show up and impose themselves in your adult life.

Ever heard the joke about the young man who calls his mother and asks her how she's feeling? With a moan, she replies, "Oh, I haven't been doing well at all." "What's wrong, Mom?" he asks. "Well, I haven't eaten for thirty days." "How come?" She replies, "Because I didn't want to have my mouth full in case you called."

Why do we laugh at that joke? Because it makes it easier for us to think about unpleasant experiences with our

3

parents, experiences we've all had and that may have had a negative impact on our emotions and behavior. In that particular joke, the young man's mother makes him feel guilty for not calling more often by showing him how hurt she is. Imagine the impact on the man in the joke if his mother had treated him this way *from childhood on up*. Maybe he'd feel guilty about not being attentive enough to her. And maybe he'd then go on and live his life . . . all his dealing with others . . . feeling it was wrong to put his needs first. Ultimately, he'd end up being angry with *himself* for doing just that. Imagine living life this way.

People often don't give much weight to the impact their parents' and siblings' guilt-provoking behaviors have on their lives. Yet the repeated comments and actions that make us think that we've wounded and threatened them just by being ourselves add up to affect us deeply. The joke above, along with its possible lifelong repercussions, makes us think that we *should* give our parents' influence more weight.

Your childhood probably had its share of carefree fun, exploring, risk-taking, sports challenges, "I dare you's" and "I double-dare you's." But "carefree fun" can quickly become "guilt-provoking events" when, for example, your parent cries out "You'll kill yourself!" as you skateboard down the hill in front of your friend's house. Or "You'll get pneumonia" when you get home from school with your jacket off and sweater tied around your waist. Then there's the "You're giving me a heart attack" when you miss the bus from the mall and get home twenty minutes later than you said you'd be home. What are the results of these repeated bombardments of parental anguish? You, the child, start believing that being carefree, playful, and adventurous threatens your parent's emotional well-being. And what do you do? As a loving child, you try to protect your very worried parent from *more* suffering by curtailing your normal childhood activities. Where does this leave you? Becoming a *grown-up* with a very cautious, inhibited attitude about sports specifically and life generally. And if it *is* sports you're overly cautious about, you'll be reluctant to ski, hike, bike; moreover, you'll have trouble overcoming your caution no matter how frustrated you feel, how hard you try, and how much you will yourself to master a sport.

Fact or Fiction? Where There's a Will There's a Way

"Where there's a will there's a way." Sound familiar? Every day I hear people dismayed at their inability to control some behavior. And they blame themselves . . . "I can't find a way to make more money," "I can't figure out how to lose more weight," "I can't understand how to have a lasting relationship." You yourself have probably made a New Year's resolution (or two, or two thousand) vowing to change something you didn't like about yourself. And you failed, right? And so you felt frustrated when you noticed you were repeating the same mistakes over and over again, and you felt panic-stricken when you realized they were the same mistakes your parents made. You felt worse knowing you'd vowed that you'd "be different" than they were when you grew up. Comedians often make us laugh about "guilt trips" our parents lay on us. But the truth is, they're no laughing matter. Their negative effects are long lasting and their guilt-provoking behaviors hold us back from achieving our dreams, whatever those dreams may be.

Guilt: The Weapon of Choice

Do you ever wonder if your parents graduated magna cum laude from Guilt University? Do you ever suspect that they majored in Suffering with a minor in Acting Out of Control? All the while earning high grades for other maneuvers that make you feel guilty instantly? I'm making light of something serious to make a point. That point is that *we keep many of these guilt-provoking examples in a place deep within us that affects our outlook, self-worth and future behavior.*

Imagine a forest alive with trees that are growing taller year by year. Then, one day, a woodsman comes in, ax in hand and swinging hard. The damage he does to the health of the forest is extreme, harsh, and long-term. Now think about these statements, some of which may sound familiar: "How could you do this to me?" WHACK! "Some day you'll realize what I've done for you!" WHACK! "I hope your children do to you what you've done to me!" TIMBER!

Just as the trees fall to the woodsman's ax, so does your ego under the blows of your parents' comments. And their damage on you is just as extreme, harsh, and long term. But just as the forest comes back to good health over time, so can you come back to your own state of health and happiness.

Communication takes many forms and so does manipulation. We've just touched on the verbal kinds of guilt-provoking examples; what about their nonverbal counterparts? Pouting. Withdrawing. Icy stares. Cold shoulders. Helpless sobbing. Forlorn looks. If all this drama is directed toward one small child, how could he or she *not* be affected?

Manipulation: Two New Varieties, Same Old Guilt

Ever experience the *Knife Twist*? How about the *Bludgeon*? Both bring you to the same place—guilt. Let's start with the parent who manipulates via "knife twisting." For the child whose parents want him or her to be excessively devoted to them, no matter how unpleasant it is, here's what may be heard around the dinner table: "I'm so miserable without you," or "How could you be so selfish and so inconsiderate of me?" or "After all I've sacrificed for you" (note this one may be accompanied by one of the already mentioned *non-verbal* "forlorn looks"). What's the effect of all this *knife twisting*? Maybe your fear of having to be *too* devoted will cause you to be afraid of close relationships and so your search for love will never end well. In the chapter "Why Can't I Fall in Love and Stay in Love," you'll read stories of people whose relationships were damaged by just this issue.

Let's continue with our other style of guilt-provoking manipulation—the *Bludgeon*. An example of this type is found when you act independently of your authoritarian parent and he or she loses control, explodes in anger, and screams at you because you weren't obedient or submissive enough. What's the effect of *bludgeoning*? In the chapter "Why Am I Fat and Why Can't I Lose Weight?" you'll read about Alice, who rebelled against her controlling parents by getting fat and staying that way.

Whether it's a slowly twisting knife, a bludgeoning from a hammer, an icy stare or a cold shoulder, the effect of these over-emotional displays of exaggerated suffering is the same— to manipulate you to change a normal behavior or abandon a normal goal. But why would you change what is normal and acceptable? Because you feel so guilty for inflicting such terrible pain, you'll conform to their personality flaws no matter how resentful or damaging that may be for *your life*.

The Stranger at the Party

As a child, it's hard to imagine that you have the power to inflict so much damage on your parents or siblings just by being yourself and doing the normal things that children do. But because they constantly act so wounded, it's difficult for you to be unaffected by their guilt-provoking behavior. Now think about this: If you had a brief encounter with an unpleasant stranger at a cocktail party, would you assume *then* that you were responsible for his offensive behavior? Or would you say to yourself, or to a friend, "What's up with him?" Chances are you'd know that if that person behaved badly, it wasn't your fault. But with your parent or sibling, you've been blamed for their unhappiness over a long, long time and you've been burdened by long-lasting feelings of (unconscious) guilt. Why is it so difficult to avoid feeling guilty toward your parents when you probably wouldn't blame yourself for the badly behaving stranger?

The Gods Must Be Angry

As children, we view our parents in the same way that members of a primitive tribe view their gods. When the gods are angry, the heavens erupt and earthquakes, floods, and droughts occur. Tribal elders know for certain that the gods must be appeased. Amends must be made for hurting the gods. With a lack of knowledge about the causes of the natural disasters it experiences, the tribe assumes that *it* has angered the gods of nature. And so by altering its behavior through prayer, performing rituals and sacrifices, the tribe believes it can placate the offended gods and so alleviate the punishment. But in altering its behavior in order to amend and atone, the tribe may make *accommodations* even if they're detrimental to its well-being—for instance, sacrificing a cow even if there's a shortage of cows.

In the same way, as a child you assumed that your behavior was responsible for provoking your parents. Though this assumption was often just a general feeling and not clearly well thought out, it *was* based on real experiences with siblings or parents who constantly acted hurt, threatened, or angered by your normal behaviors. Remember the mother in the joke at the beginning of the chapter—the one who made her son feel guilty about not paying enough attention to her? Have you ever been in a similar situation? If so, what did you do? Did you act like the member of the indigenous tribe and make sacrifices to appease your gods (okay, *parents*)? Did you change something normal in yourself in order to not hurt them again? Was the result that you resented yourself for appeasing your parents at your own expense? If so, your resentment will also have you trapped in self-defeating responses as you go through life. What might that look like? You might rebel against the mother in the joke and become unresponsive to *anyone* who wants your interest. Or, in response to a controlling parent, you might become stubborn, defiant, and disagreeable, no matter how severe the cost is to you. Throughout your life these qualities will undermine your relationships with others and also your goals.

Congratulations, You've Been Hired by Mystery Firm X

Changing to keep your parents happy, or at least to *not* make them angry, is something you may have tried while growing up. But did you know exactly *what* you were changing and *why*? And if you didn't, did you still try to change anyway? Compare your situation to this one and see if it helps put it all in perspective for you.

You've been job-hunting for a while and now at last your search is over. You've landed a job. Only problem is, you don't know what the job entails, what is expected of you, and what the requirements actually are. One day you walk into work and your boss is angry with you and you don't know why. You find yourself thinking, "What did I do?" "Was it the way I handled report A, was it the way I dealt with situation B, or maybe it was how I dealt with customer C?" You decide which situation you think it was and then you make what you think is the appropriate change. Next time, you think (and hope) it will be different. Your boss will have nothing to be angry about. You've taken care of the problem. Does that make sense to you? Changing, but not knowing what you did wrong or fully understanding the situation before you started to make the change? If you don't know what the problem is, how can you possibly be expected to fix it? To an adult this probably doesn't make sense, does it? But this is what we, as kids, do. Right or wrong, sense or *non*sense, we try to change to make sure our parents (or other siblings) won't be angry or hurt. We're always trying to keep those "gods" of ours *happy* so they don't get *angry*.

Guilt, Resentment, and Our Struggles

There is a profound connection between the feelings of guilt and resentment and the problems you struggle with: sex, money, weight, ambition, relationships, and parenting. A deeper understanding of these feelings will help you solve these problems.

Why Do I Feel Guilty?

Before we can start to understand the *why* behind the guilt, let's first define it. Guilt means that we believe that something we are doing is causing pain to someone else. It's activated by our behavior, thoughts, or feelings that we judge to be wrong or bad.

Normal parents are protective of their children. But what if your parents were *over*protective? What if every time you played sports, rode your bike, or roughhoused with friends, your parent—at best—became disturbed and—at worst—frantic? "Watch out, you'll get hurt!" "You'll break a leg!" and so on. Would you have interpreted that as interest in your well-being, or rather, believed that you were hurting your parents by your sense of adventure and fun? Children who think that their actions are causing pain for their parents will feel guilt.

Let me be clear. I'm *not* talking about a parent's *normal* range of caution and concern. I *am* talking about *extreme* caution and worry over small risks. But if you grew up always experiencing irrational guilt about worrying an overprotective parent, you'll also experience guilt in response to risks as an adult. You'll feel frustrated by your excessive sense of caution, but most likely you won't be aware of its cause, and so you'll be unable to change.

Does Any of This Sound Familiar?

1. You feel responsible for your parents' or siblings' misery, and guilty about pursuing your own goals. How you tried placating them, or atoning, in order to relieve your sense of guilt will explain some of your self-defeating life patterns.

2. You quietly developed self-hatred and resentment about having to inhibit a normal behavior or goal when your parent continuously behaved badly toward you. How did you respond to the resentment you felt?

3. You rebelled as a way of protesting. You hoped that they'd get the message you were sending by your behavior and change for the better (that is, you became stubborn to protest against a parent who was too controlling in the hopes that he or she would get the message and be less controlling). *Or* you rebelled to prove to yourself that you're your own person and you can't

be manipulated. This type of *defiant* rebelliousness is responsible for many painful self-defeating behaviors.

4. Even though you promised yourself that when you grew up you'd never behave the way your parents did with you, you notice that you're mimicking their worst qualities.

I want you to know why it's so hard to free ourselves of the behaviors we hate no matter how hard we try, no matter how much willpower we exert, no matter how much advice we receive from others. To understand why it *is* so hard, we'll delve into why our childhood patterns continue on into our adult lives even though they are clearly negative patterns and we no longer are living with our parents. The negative effects of our family experiences remain hidden from our conscious mind, even though this information is critical to changing what we most dislike about ourselves. We'll pin down this elusive awareness in this book and you'll begin to make positive changes in your negative behaviors. Finally and amazingly, many people you'll meet will tell you that they didn't experience major problems in their families and they aren't aware of *any* guilt feelings. And they'll tell you this despite obvious, and serious, personal problems. Why? Let's see.

Exercise: Now Look at Yourself

Imagine that you could be reborn into your family today. Now imagine that you were born into your family with all the knowledge that you possess *right now*. Consider writing about the following:

- What would be different for you in your relationship with your mother?
- What would be different for you in your relationship with your father?

- What would be different for you in your relationship with your siblings?

Moving Ahead

Beginning the process of change means beginning a hunt for the causes of your problems that are lurking below the surface of any problem. In Chapter 2 we'll start the hunt for your underlying causes.

CHAPTER 2

Do You Think You're in Control of Your Life?

You've got the talent, you've got the ability, so why can't you overcome your problems? You're highly motivated to change, but you still can't seem to stop behaving in ways you hate. You have excellent problem-solving skills, yet you can't solve the personal ones that plague you the most. You know that if you do your job well, you'll probably get a raise and/or a promotion, yet you go ahead and sabotage it. You know that if you're considerate of people you'll be well liked, yet you can't stop being rude. You know that if you're careful about saving and investing your money you'll probably enjoy a prosperous retirement, yet you spend carelessly. Why can't you figure out how to change your behavior and so change your life? Why, if what you're doing is making you unhappy, can't you stop doing it?

When we have problems that we can't seem to solve, many of us start thinking that we're lazy, inexperienced, or maybe even unintelligent. We do this because it's too scary for us to conclude the alternative. What *is* the alternative? That it may not be possible for us to be in control of our lives. If it were so easy to be in control, wouldn't we all just do it? Make the change, stop the pain, live happily?

Free Choice: Do You
Really Have It?

This question of whether or not you actually possess free will
has been a hot topic for a long, long time. From theologians to
philosophers to the parents of teenagers, the question has been
discussed and debated ad infinitum. Why? Because free choice
and compulsive self-defeating behavior coexist in all of us.

Who Is Fighting for
Control of Your Soul?

It's not only God and the Devil who may be fighting for control of your soul—you're right in there too. When you can't
believe that you're behaving just like your parent did—even
though you promised yourself that you'd be different when
you were a parent yourself—you are entering the fray. People
usually assume that they can control their lives because much
of the time, by following good advice, by applying rational
strategies, or by appreciating the lessons from past experience, they *do* in fact succeed. Yet, at the same time, many of
us also recognize that our free will is limited. We recognize
this most often when we come face to face with an example
of our self-defeating behavior and we know that this behavior hasn't budged even though we've done our best to overcome it. Which leads me to ask . . .

Willpower and Self-Interest:
Enough to Make You Change?

When a magazine presents you with "Five Easy Steps to Losing
Weight," when an audio series offers "Four Tapes to
Investment Success," and a TV personality does back-to-back
shows on "The Ins & Outs of Good Parenting," you know

that if you actually had control over life, achieving these goals and improving your life would be as simple as buying a subscription, purchasing some tapes, or turning on the TV. Nice and easy, right? Don't we wish. But what happens when we do all of the above and we wind up failing anyway? What are we left to believe about ourselves? "I'm lazy." "I'm stupid." "I'm a screwup." But here's something to think about. Were you "lazy" when you were looking for a date on a computer dating service and you went through hundreds of potential matches? Is that what a "lazy" person does? Were you a screwup when you wanted a job and went out and made sure you got the right training to do it well? Is that what a "screwup" does? And when it came to learning how to use your new computer and you managed just fine, was that being "stupid"? So actually, those reasons won't work with you across the board, will they? Then what will? Because it is getting pretty frustrating not being able to use your intelligence, your energy, your determination to succeed in all areas of your life. The solution exists and it lies in our hidden self-destructive motivations.

If you could understand the nature of your hidden negative motivations, you could use that information to change. What if you had an illness, but you didn't know it was caused by a specific germ? Your suffering could be long and needless because you might not know which of the available antibiotics was the right one to take. Or, let's say you wanted to make yourself more attractive but you lived in a world without mirrors. It would be difficult for you to know what to do. Did you need to improve you hair, your complexion, or your teeth or your skin? These examples show us the important concept: *to solve any problem and change your life . . . look for the underlying causes.*

People want to be successful and happy in life. Period. So if you find yourself behaving in ways that you hate, getting

bad reactions from people around you, and having little success using willpower and advice to change those actions,
wouldn't it seem that something *beyond your control* is dic-
tating your actions?

You're like a well-made ship piloted by a captain who
forgot to bring the navigation charts on the voyage. All of the
captain's successes in other areas of his life won't help him on
this particular voyage. So let's roll out our own ship's charts
and see how to navigate the choppy seas of our lives, starting
with a little knowledge about . . .

The Major Behaviors We Hate

You've probably seen some of these very common and very frustrating behaviors in people you know and in characters in movies
you've seen and books you've read, beginning with . . .

I'LL START TOMORROW (WELL, MAYBE THE DAY AFTER TOMORROW)

Are you one of those people who seem very comfortable with
self-defeating acts in the moment? But later, when the moment has passed, do you hate yourself for behaving that way?
Do you know anyone (including yourself) who indulges a pas-
sion for desserts no matter what the cost? Do you wonder
why his or her (or your?) sense of regret doesn't lead to different eating choices the next time? Do you (or anyone you
know) distract yourself from important tasks such as schoolwork or a job by partying, watching TV, daydreaming, and
so on, and then justify it to yourself or others? It may feel
great at the time, but the remorse that inevitably follows is
like that killer hangover that also fails to motivate constructive changes. When you promise yourself to do better the next
time—as you do when you say "I'll start my diet next week"
and you still fail to follow through—you're left with a strong

sense of betrayal, remorse, and guilt for having failed . . . yet again.

ARE YOUR FANTASIES A SUBSTITUTE FOR REAL SATISFACTION?

Are your fantasies the major source of your happiness? Think about your weight fantasies, your relationship fantasies, your sex fantasies, your fantasies about power, parenting, money, and success. If you want to make your fantasies become realities, you need to change. Pick your dream. Go ahead. Is it a dream of being powerful, admired, creative, great in bed, wealthy, the world's best parent? We all have dreams—nothing wrong with that and nothing too surprising either. What is surprising is how often these dreams remain out of reach to us despite our great desire to achieve them and despite knowing that our happiness depends on fulfilling them.

LOVE, SEX, AND ROMANCE, OR WHY YOU CAN'T GET NO SATISFACTION

Remember your fantasies about acquiring great sexual power, appeal, and success like movie stars? Remember your dreams of great everlasting love from the protagonists of romance novels? As adults, if these fantasies don't become transformed into realistic life satisfactions, it's a sign of serious underlying conflicts. Does that mean that perfect beauty and/or a buff physique are necessary for happiness? No. We all probably know people who are average in looks but very powerful in sex appeal. And there are those who are well endowed with looks but are inept at romance and love. The important question is, how and why do we fall short, and why is it so difficult to change?

Here are some common signs of underlying trouble. You're great at seducing someone, but run the other way as soon as he or she falls in love with you. You lose interest in sex with a willing, attractive, and sexy partner, yet there was no such problem in the beginning of the relationships. You need pornography, or fantasies with someone else, or fantasies of your partner having sex with someone else in order to get aroused. You need a good fight with your spouse as a prelude to sex. If you notice that any of these issues apply to you, you'll soon learn what's behind these patterns, and how to use that information to overcome them.

SEXUAL AFFAIRS, OR NEVER GETTING TOO INVOLVED WITH ONE PERSON

What do you think motivates someone to have affairs when it can be so completely detrimental to one's well-being? You may say that the person who is engaging in the affair feels excited, or is having a great adventure, but in fact the behavior is usually truly self-destructive. The chapter "Why Can't I Fall in Love or Stay in Love" will explain why so many people have affairs instead of serious long-term relationships.

ANOTHER BAD RELATIONSHIP, OR WHEN WILL I EVER LEARN?

For many of us, it's hard to understand the motivation of people who complain about partners who mistreat them but don't stand up for themselves and/or leave. You yourself may notice that you have an ability to attract a desirable partner, but then become critical of him or her.

Why, you wonder, do you (or others) choose partners with qualities that seem so mismatched with your (their) own? What do you make of the shy person married to a domineering person? Ever wonder how you'd be affected if you needed to have everything in its place but were married to a disorganized slob? Why make that choice in the first place?

As you read on and start recognizing a few simple principles, you'll find that it's becoming much easier to figure out the choices you and others make.

WHEN SUCCESS AND MONEY ELUDE YOU, OR I COULDA BEEN A CONTENDER

Failure to achieve success, to make their ambitions come true, is a major source of distress for a lot of people. Does career or school success elude you completely, or do you undermine yourself *after* you achieve success at work or school?

Perhaps you dropped out of school even though you wanted to be someone? Maybe you're a perennial student who's afraid to graduate into the real work world? Or maybe you can't reach your professional goals despite having talent to spare and opportunities waiting? So what's the problem? Is it possible that your problems with success revolve around money? Many people habitually lose money when investing, even though they have years of experience in the market and have read everything on the subject. Do you have similar problems with money and success?

Have you ever noticed that after accomplishing academic, career, or financial goals, some people become increasingly anxious or depressed? Have you ever seen someone avoid taking credit for the successful outcome of a big project while attributing the success to others or to simple "good luck"? Do you find it ironic that the happiness normally associated with personal achievement is replaced by worry, unhappiness, or excessive modesty? Sometimes problems with success and money are really about the following two issues, best summed up as: Why Am I Such a Wimp? And I'm a Worthless Nobody. Let's tackle the wimp issue first.

WHY AM I SUCH A WIMP, OR A LACK OF ASSERTIVENESS AND POWER

Think of the word "power." What comes to mind? Is it a picture of an influential person who realizes his or her goals, leads organizations, garners respect, and gains admiration? Why is it that for some people, personal power seems to fail them at every turn of their lives? A lack of personal power doesn't just show up at work or at home, it rears its head in the most unexpected places, too.

When you're susceptible to sales people who want you to buy products that you don't really want and definitely don't need, your lack of personal power is showing. When you can't turn down requests for money, or conversely, you say no to any and all requests and suggestions—oops, it's your lack of personal power again. How do you explain people who always act self-sacrificing and can't help but put others' needs first? Yes, you've got it, it's that pesky lack of personal power. Now let's go on and see about this "worthless nobody."

WHY AM I A WORTHLESS NOBODY?

Many people are plagued by negative behaviors and thoughts that affect their ability to be liked and to feel good about themselves. Does this sound familiar—you can't accept a compliment, and you're unable to let yourself be the center of attention? Then there are people who criticize themselves excessively. Ever encountered thoughts like this in yourself? "I'm a baby." (For "baby" you can substitute words like "no good," "lazy," "stupid," and a whole host of others.) Once you have the word in your head, is it hard to get it *out* of your head? If so, you can consider yourself to be a member of the "Worthless Nobody Club." Not one you probably want to be a member of, and one that we'll deal with in greater detail later. When we do, you may find ways to resign your membership from the club and move on.

ARE YOUR LITTLE ANGELS
LITTLE DEVILS IN DISGUISE?

Anyone who has raised children knows how often you can be blindsided by their unexpected behaviors, behaviors that provoke you and are difficult for you to deal with. Some of these exasperating actions are normal parts of a child's early development, like acting cooperatively, then immediately afterward refusing to do what you want, or like getting very close to you, only to reject you one minute later for the other parent, and like turning to you for comfort, love, and advice, then ignoring you.

If you are overly sensitive to any of these behaviors, and react by acting hurt or threatened, it will cause your children to behave in more extreme and more provoking ways. Chapter 16, "I've Become My Mother/Father and My Child Is a Pain," addresses the question, Why do some of these patterns become increasingly rigid and unyielding as some children get older (especially during adolescence)? Why does this happen no matter how frustrated, angry, pleading, or cajoling you become, no matter how many rewards you promise? You find yourself wondering "What's gotten into them?" as if they've become possessed by the devil, or as if one of the plagues sent down on the Pharaoh was visited upon you instead.

The key to overcoming these problems is to understand which one of *your* behaviors (hidden from your awareness) is responsible for the behavior that you can't stand in your child. This book will help you identify which of your words and your deeds are responsible, and then will show you how to use this information to help them get on track.

THE NEW SEE FOOD DIET, OR EATING EVERYTHING YOU SEE

Everyone who has had a weight problem at some time in his or her life can appreciate how difficult it can be to keep under control. In spite of the abundance of diets that prevail, a large number of people continue to overeat and hate themselves for it. If this is the case, then clearly there must be some hidden self-defeating motivations that are responsible for the compulsive habit of overeating in spite of "best intentions." In the chapter "Why Am I Fat and Why Can't I Lose Weight?"

I'll describe the six underlying reasons for this. If this is one of your own problems, reading on will help you discover which motive applies to you.

WHY CAN'T YOU GET YOUR ACT TOGETHER, OR SO YOU THINK YOU LEFT HOME?

Why does behavior we hate that originates in childhood continue far into adult life when we're not even living with our family? If we're no long under the influence of our parents or our siblings, why are we still controlled by the self-defeating beliefs that have their roots with them? Later in this book, I'll show you a chart called "How You Create New Moral Codes to Live By" and you'll understand how you create new moral codes for yourself. The codes or rules are all based on experiences you had while dealing with your parents' and/or your siblings' flaws.

Exercise: Now Look at Yourself

Looking back over this chapter, did you have a particularly strong reaction when we mentioned the "major behaviors we hate"? Here they are again, and as you reread them, please note your response to each one. If your response is neutral, mark the item with an "N." If it has an emotional charge, if it grabs you by the throat, if it feels like a sock in the stomach, give it a number from 1 to 5 (1 packs the least punch, 5 packs a wallop). Next to the ones you gloss over very, very quickly, the ones you want to ignore, put a star. Here is the list of the 11 behaviors we hate in ourselves:

1. I'll Start Tomorrow (Well, Maybe the Day after Tomorrow)

2 Are Your Fantasies a Substitute for Real Satisfaction?

3. Love, Sex, and Romance, or Why You Can't Get No Satisfaction

4. Sexual Affairs, or Never Getting Too Involved with One Person

5. Another Bad Relationship, or When Will I Ever Learn?

6. When Success and Money Elude You, or I Coulda Been a Contender

7. Why Am I Such a Wimp, or a Lack of Assertiveness and Power

8. Why Am I a Worthless Nobody?

9. Are Your Little Angels Little Devils in Disguise?

10. The New See Food Diet, or Eating Everything You See

11. Why Can't You Get Your Act Together, or So You Think You Left Home?

That's all for now. We're just trying to create an opening up of your awareness to these behaviors in yourself, and that's plenty for the present moment.

Moving Ahead

We've just introduced different behaviors that are probably affecting your life and in ways that aren't good for you. Guilt and rebellion lie behind them. In the next chapter we're going to look at guilt and rebellion from a different angle. We'll see how they stick their hooks into you early on and then hold on tight throughout your life. Understanding this is a big step toward removing the hooks and moving on.

CHAPTER 3

Guilt and Rebellion: Whose Life Is It Anyway?

Do you ever feel you're not in control of your own life? Do you ever wonder who *is,* and how they got to hold down that all-important job? Let's try to crack the secret code of who's in control. Once we do you'll see how it will help you live your life more successfully and become less self-defeating and more in charge of all that affects you.

Say Hello to Those Twin String Pullers

A situation has just arisen and you've responded to it in a way that is over the top and completely inappropriate. In fact, your response was so out of character you catch yourself thinking, "What was *that* about?" Or maybe, "*Who was* that person who just acted like that?" So there you go, you've just encountered the twin string pullers, guilt and rebellion. They are the two keys here. They get their grip on you early and hold on tightly throughout your life. They cause you to respond to situations in ways that feel foreign to you. How does it happen?

Have you ever had to deal with a broken thermostat? With no warning at all it automatically turns your heater way up, and then, at precisely the wrong time, and again with no warning whatsoever, it shuts it off. Your damaged control system functions in much the same way, thanks in no small part to guilt and rebellion. It includes your beliefs, feelings, and all the rules that have become ingrained over the course of your life. And not so much because of anything you yourself have done, but more because of those unresolved problems and issues of your parents (and sometimes siblings) and their effect on you.

"Always Be Nice to Others"

This is a common rule that many of us heard growing up, and on the surface it seems like a rule that would cause us no harm. But it may affect us in our adult life in ways that are detrimental. Let's have a look.

Being nice to others sounds like a great value to possess. What could possibly be wrong with it? It has a positive moral value for those who hold it. Most people are able to choose when it's appropriate to be nice and, when it's actually harmful to their well-being, to refuse to be nice. But for the person who suffers from excessive guilt about breaking this rule, it becomes a trap.

Let's say your parent or sibling was long-suffering and required you to always put aside your needs for the needs of others. Any attempt on your part to be self-serving in a very normal, typical way resulted in injurious remarks or maybe even physical abuse. Frequently, comments were heard like, "How could you be so selfish and ignore your suffering mother?" or "Your only brother, your own flesh and blood, needs your help on the computer and all you can think about is writing your college essay and getting into college?" What was all that about, you may wonder? Guilt.

Guilt has required that you be excessively devoted to others at the expense of your own interests. And if you aren't able to oppose the rule "always be nice to others," and your damaged inner thermostat is of no help when you're trying to determine whether a person truly deserves your being nice to him or her, you become a slave to that simple rule.

How does it play out in your life today? You become a doormat to others. You often feel exploited and unappreciated. And what happens if you wake up one day hating yourself for acting so submissively to people? (And the actual process of "waking up" could take years, not just a morning, though that could happen too.) You become a person who defiantly responds to all requests with "No." This includes reasonable requests as well, like taking your brother to a basketball game that you were actually looking forward to. But the new you, the one who must rebel against his or her past, rebels against the request and doesn't go. Won't go. Period. End of story.

But is it really the end or is it perhaps the middle of the story? Your story can end with how you turned your life around, how you re-routed yourself on a road map established early in your childhood which led you away from the best road to follow. Now you have a chance to take a new road, which is the best road, and lead a life in which *you* are the one in control.

The Gods Must Be Angry . . . But Is It My Fault?

Remember the indigenous tribe I mentioned earlier? The one that faced natural disasters like earthquakes, floods, and droughts? With no scientific explanations, the tribe used its own logic, "We've angered the gods and we must atone." These powerful feelings of guilt require atonement or punishment, and they require that the tribe pay a price for assuming blame.

And so must you. Surprised? It's not a big stretch actually, not if you think of your family as its own tribe with its own set of rules and rituals. And as it does for the faraway tribe, trouble comes when you rebel against the gods (or, in your case, your parents).

When you're a child, you often blame yourself for the serious flaws of your parents' (and siblings') behavior. Even though these flaws are not your fault, you still feel compelled to placate them. And you will do so even at great cost to yourself. Remember the basketball-loving sibling who said an emphatic "No" to the request to take his brother to a basketball game? Who lost out there? What was the cost of his behavior? He missed out on something that brings fun, excitement, and a good time into his life. Self-defeating behavior? You bet.

Why Do I Do It If It Makes Me Unhappy?

It's called *placating behavior,* and while it may cause you to be unhappy, it also makes a lot of sense in the scheme of family things. When, as a child, our NBA fan assumed responsibility for the misbehaviors of his parent, he accommodated his parent's flaw ("always be nice to others"). He did this hoping to make things okay with his parent so that the parent would stop making him feel bad if he followed his own path. That's the *adaptive* purpose of his behavior. Like the indigenous tribe, he too tried to appease the gods (parents) to make sure the same things didn't happen again.

As a child, he probably found it very hard to *not* accommodate his parent's flaws. Quite possibly because the "guilt trips" that were imposed on him were powerful, painful, and like a wrestler's forceful armhold, they made the child submit to their demands. But when we hold onto our tribe's personal beliefs (inner rules) too tightly and always try to obey them, we often end up behaving in destructive ways. Yet when we try to ignore them and take a stab at doing what is in our best interests, we often end up experiencing strong feelings of guilt.

That age old "damned if you do, damned if you don't" fits perfectly into this scenario. You hate yourself for giving in to these negative inner rules (always be nice to others) just as you hate yourself for giving in to the irrational, negative behaviors of your parents. What does that leave you with? Resentment. Where does resentment take you?

To fighting against having to give in to these rules, or defiance. What's another word for defiance? *Rebellion.* And what's the title of this chapter? Guilt and *Rebellion.* Ah, it's starting to click now, isn't it? And as crazy as it seems (but then again, remember those "gods"—we said they "must be angry" and it turns out, they're crazy, too) we can be forced against our will to adopt the *very same qualities* of our parents that we hated. And although most of us vow to act better, or at least, *differently,* than our parents did when we were growing up, many of us notice that we have actually assumed their worst qualities.

Arriving Where We Began and Knowing It for the First Time

Which brings us back to our opening question, "Why aren't you in control of your life?" Now that we can see *and* understand why you aren't in control, the only question left to answer is, "How can I *be* in control of my life?" And you can be.

If you find yourself behaving in ways that you hate and feel unable to change, you're probably acting according to unconscious destructive mental rules. It's as if you've become your very own computer virus. And like a computer virus, which conveys misinformation and causes your computer to act in self-destructive ways, these "*self*-viruses" interfere with your goals, fulfillment, and happiness and cause you to act in self-destructive ways too. How do you clear out the virus? Is there a Norton Anti-Virus that can scan your brain's files and documents and rid it of the affected ones so that you run smoothly and up to speed for the rest of your days? It'd be nice if it were that simple, and while it isn't, there *are* ways to make fulfillment, success, and happiness a part of your future inner computer program.

Practical, Meet Impractical. Simple, Meet Complicated

It's time for me to take off my author's hat and replace it with my psychiatrist's. Solving long-standing behavioral problems, past problems that affect our present-day lives, is something that usually takes time and a lot of work. However, I also believe that there are things you can do today, things you can carry through with tomorrow and the days to come, that will begin the process. In the section that follows, "Exercise: Now Look at Yourself," you're going to address what I call practical approaches to some very impractical problems.

Exercise: Now Look at Yourself

Take out your pen and paper, or create a new document on your computer. It doesn't matter which; what does matter is that you do it. What are we doing? We're making a list of your "Impractical Problems." To get you started I'll give you two examples.

Impractical Problem #1

I like to watch sports on TV on the weekends.

Why is that a problem? My wife/girlfriend doesn't like to.

What new problem does that create? We fight.

What bigger problem does that create? I don't enjoy watching sports on TV.

What other problem does that create? I feel badly when I watch.

What's running through my head? I'm selfish.

Have I heard that before? If so, where?

Impractical Problem #2

In the above example you and your wife or girlfriend fight over your interest in watching sports on TV, but you insist on doing it.

What problem does that create? I feel uncomfortable watching sports on TV.

What other problem does it create? She pulls away from me.

What's running through my head? I'm stubborn as a mule. No one tells me what to do.

Moving Ahead

You're starting to get an idea of whose voice it is you hear in the back of your head at different times and in different situations, and that's good. It will allow you to understand what you grew up hearing and how it continues to affect you today. Underlying causes of behaviors affect you—there's no doubt about that. And those causes can also be changed. But only when you identify them. Congratulations. By doing the above exercise you've just identified one, maybe two, maybe more underlying causes, and you're on your way to long-lasting change.

In Chapter 4 you'll start seeing how you made it through your family in one piece by acting and behaving in certain ways. But you probably don't like these ways anymore (that's why you're reading this book), and you think they may be holding you back today, so let's continue to unearth the reasons we behave in ways we hate.

CHAPTER 4

Surviving Your Family

Are you starting to see the outline of the puzzle taking shape? When completed, the puzzle will reveal how we are negatively affected by guilt and resentment. What are some other mental motivations that are influenced by guilt, resentment, and pain? How do these motivations contribute to the behaviors that plague us? Once you see how these work, it will be a lot easier to understand the different motivations for any major problem that you find yourself wrestling with . . . over and over again.

There are mechanisms you've developed to "survive your family." The core workings of them are behind the behaviors you have and don't like. The big three mechanisms are accommodation, rebellion, and mimicking. Once you understand why you've invited them into your life and made them so comfortable over the years, you'll start seeing that you can also ask them to leave. Once gone, the behaviors that seemed impossible *to* change *will* change.

Accommodation

What's another way of saying accommodation? Try this: *placing your parent or sibling before you at your own expense.* To maintain the important ties to our parents or siblings, to feel loved by them, we may *accommodate to* or *comply with* their reasonable expectations. That's okay, right? Sure, but what about accommodating or complying with their serious flaws and damaging expectations? Not as "okay," right? Too much accommodation causes us to ignore our own interests, goals, and destiny. If that were the case, why would we do this? *Because their guilt-provoking words and deeds show us that they're hurt when we don't comply or accommodate.*

Huh? Look at it like this: Say you become very obedient to a very controlling parent; you could easily become too submissive and you could quickly learn to squelch your own independent thinking. What happens if you don't comply? Usually, this kind of parent becomes agitated—he screams, she loses control, maybe they become violent. What does he scream? "You damn kid. You never listen. Do it now or I'm going to kill you!" Their insults, screaming, and other such behaviors are all clear evidence that your parents are fragile. You've wounded them. You've sent them right over the edge. So what's a nice, well-meaning kid supposed to do? How about limiting his or her normal sense of independence?

Accommodation or compliance is very likely to cause you to suffer profoundly if your submissive behavior continues for the rest of your life. You'll hate yourself for not asserting yourself and then you'll find that people close to you can't stand you for the very same reason. Maybe you'll try to suppress it and it just comes out anyway. Every time you come in late for a meeting, stubbornly disagree with everyone around you, or even do an assignment with begrudging defiance, you're revealing your resentment of your authoritarian parent.

ACCOMMODATION—AND SUCCESS

Do you know people who can't enjoy any success they have in their career? Does it not make any sense to you when you see them unable to bask in the light of their achievements? It may make sense if you understood their family life growing up. Here is one example: a parent who lived through the children's accomplishments, and needed for them to be perfect in everything they did. And so, good grades were never good enough. What would a 90 percent on a test ensure? Endless criticism, a clutching of the chest in disbelief, and bitter complains.

And what would the child's response be to all of this? The belief that if she weren't perfect, she'd ruin her parents' life. What behaviors would it cause in such children? They'd become driven, feeling that no matter how much they achieved, it was never enough. Where would that lead? To the inability to enjoy any achievement, to never be able to relax, have fun, and do any activity for the pleasure of it because to do so would make them feel guilty. Unconsciously, they assume that their parent will feel devastated if they're not always seeking to achieve more. And more and more.

ACCOMMODATION—AND RELATIONSHIPS

Do any people you know, friends perhaps, have trouble getting close to someone they're strongly attracted to? Looked at from the outside in, it may not make a lot of sense, but looked at from the inside, it probably does. What if a friend had a parent who was extremely needy, who absolutely had to be in full possession of your friend's love and attention? Your friend's closeness to this parent was essential for the parent's well-being, so much so that he or she would resent your friend's normal involvement with others. Sulking, acting depressed and moody when your friend was happy or close to anyone else (including teachers, grandparents, or friends) were well within the repertoire of this parent's behavior whenever your friend was spending time with others.

Finding fault with anyone your friend valued was another sign that the parent felt wounded by the child. What was the effect of all of this on your friend? An obligation to change his or her personality just to maintain a relationship to the parent: staying tied to the apron strings, complimenting the parent all the time, showing extra affection, spending less time with friends. All are possible coping mechanisms developed by your friend to accommodate this parent's possessive need for him or her. "Loyalty" will become a high priority moral value in your friend's mind, and it will have a powerful influence throughout his or her life.

And the effect of this particular accommodation on future relationships will be detrimental at best, dysfunctional at worst. Your friend will either feel uncomfortable pursuing friends for fear of being disloyal to his parent, or he'll worry that anyone he's seriously involved with will require undue loyalty and devotion from him.

This is how accommodation can start, and it is also the start of some people's self-defeating motivations. In the case study below, we'll see how one man's accommodation affected his ability to succeed in business and in relationships.

▨ ALEX ▨

Alex was driven by guilt. He was a forty-year-old financial planner who gave in to almost all requests made of him by friends and clients. However, his loudest complaint about himself centered on his inability to refuse people's requests for loans. He resented this tendency in himself, but mere self-resentment wasn't enough to make him resist lending them money. Alex told me that he wanted to overcome this "terrible" habit of his.

At the same time, Alex was in emotional turmoil over a serious relationship. Although attracted to Gina, he was very anxious about getting involved with her. He had felt the same anxiety with previous women he had dated. Alex had no idea why he was so fearful. He didn't know that his tendency to give in to people (accommodate) was the cause of this anxiety too.

Talking to Alex, I learned that his mother had totally controlled his life. Absolute compliance to her wishes was required of Alex. If he didn't please her, she'd become sad, act hurt, and would sometimes complain that Alex didn't love her enough. The effect on Alex? The belief that it was wrong to disappoint her. Guilt, when he did. The stage was set for Alex's lifelong pattern of giving in to others.

And Gina? The close relationship he was developing with her made him feel very anxious because *unconsciously* Alex assumed that he'd have to be totally compliant to Gina as he was to everyone else.

How the two were so intimately connected was one of the things that Alex wanted to understand better. Alex began to assess his irrational behavior of accommodating people's requests by comparing his childhood responses to his mother with the ones he currently had with his clients and his girlfriend. Doing so eventually helped Alex become more and more comfortable about refusing people's requests for money.

The surprise for Alex was that his clients didn't take offense or fire him when he started turning down their financial requests. Instead, they seemed to respect him more. And Gina? As Alex became more comfortable disagreeing with her, he started to become more involved with her and closer to her too.

YOU'RE STUCK

Did you ever have a terribly painful blind date—one that, thankfully, only lasted a short time? Now think about your childhood situation. You're stuck with your parents and siblings for years and years, no matter what. Now think of the accumulated resentment building up after years of accommodating behaviors that you know shifted you away from some of your normal qualities and goals. To relieve this resentment, you may have become an accommodator, like Alex. Another route you could have taken was *rebellion*. What does that look like and how does it show up in your life? Let's see.

Rebellion (the Opposite of Accommodation)

What's another way of saying rebellion? *Refusal to comply with parental demands or needs and the restrictions they impose.* Yes, it's true that a certain amount of rebellion is normal and healthy in the development of a child's independence and control. But once again, when a parent's expectations are extreme, that child will rebel against accommodating his or her parents in order to fight their attempts to limit the normal goals we set for ourselves.

Children aren't usually able to complain *to* their parents about *how* their parents' specific behavior is spoiling their life. When was the last time you heard a young daughter complaining to her father, "Dad, your behavior is ruining my psychosocial development." Right: never. So, rebellion, as a protest, is meant to *signal, or communicate,* to parents that their actions are not just distressing, but they need to stop— period. And that would be fine if not for one problem: Parents have their own hidden self-defeating motivations from their *own* childhoods. Do these cause them to keep behaving badly? You bet it does. Does it also prevent them from receiving their child's message in a mature way? Right again. Ultimately, parents' unresolved childhood issues wind up provoking them even more and the cycle of parent/child conflict continues unchanged. Let's look at another case study. It's the real-life story of Will, a stubborn man who used rebellion as a way of acting out against his parents' demands.

▨ **WILL** ▨

Will was looking for more control. He was a wealthy businessman who refused almost all requests made of him by his wife, Tracy. Any time Tracy asked for, suggested, or requested something, Will's response was always the same, "No!" Whether her suggestion was important or meaningless, Will's negative response never wavered. Why did he do this, despite the fact that he was really provoking Tracy? Because Will was rebelling against his strong impulses to accommodate others. A devastating combination of parental traits created in Will a strong inclination towards giving in to others. Let's look at his father first.

Authoritarian and pompous, he required Will to accept his point of view and to give in to his orders, and if Will didn't, his father would react angrily. Comments like, "What's wrong with you?" "Why are you so thick headed?" "Listen to me, I have years of experience and I know what I'm talking about," dominated Will's childhood. Will's father needed to be completely in charge, and although Will viewed that as a sign of weakness, he still complied with the needs of his father to maintain his father's position of authority and self-importance. He did this by agreeing with and doing whatever his father expected of him.

Now, for his mother, Will was a confidant and companion. Because her husband was uninterested in her (which she confided to Will), Will felt obliged to cheer her up and spend time with her. He did this so she wouldn't feel lonely or unhappy. Pressure from both parents left Will unable to do what made him happy. If he did, he felt he'd hurt his parents because he wasn't focusing on their needs. And so, Will grew up feeling that his role was to accommodate everyone else's wants.

To make himself feel that he was more in control of his life (and not be the wimp who complied with everyone else's demands), Will, without even being aware of it, developed a protective, stubborn quality of automatically saying no to people's wishes, even if they seemed reasonable. This was the opposite of Alex's way of accommodating everyone.

Will complained, when he came to see me, that he and his wife fought all the time. He said he couldn't stand Tracy because she was too demanding and critical of him. Will had no awareness that his lifelong inclination to give in to people, which we now know started back with his parents, was behind his problem with Tracy. Any request from her was viewed as dangerous because he (unconsciously) worried about having to submit to her and become her servant. And the problem wasn't just confined to his marriage, either. Every relationship caused him anxiety about having to become a slave to the other person's requests.

Becoming more aware of the source of his problem, Will began realizing that he equated *reasonable requests* with the *unpleasant demands* of his parents. Therefore, he wasn't able to rationally evaluate his wife's requests and suggestions. Will gained understanding of his problem, and the effect was an increasing relative comfort with saying no to Tracy when he meant it and saying yes when that was the appropriate response.

Soon they began fighting less. Disagreements now took on new meaning for Will. They no longer served only the purpose of fighting against giving in. Now they could also reflect his actual point of view.

NO RELIEF

When children fight against excessively accommodating the flaws of their parents and siblings, they suffer so much guilt for their rebellion that they resume accommodating in order to *relieve* their guilt. Where does that leave them? Shifting back and forth between two evils and never finding relief.

Mimicking

When you were a child you probably remember swearing to the universe that when you grew up you'd never, ever treat your children the way your parents treated you. You'd be different; you'd be better. You knew it from the core of your being. Right? So how is it that instead of making your vow come true, all these years later you've ended up copying their very qualities that you most despised? Welcome to the world of mimicking—the third mechanism (*accommodation* and *rebellion* being the other two) we sometimes use that's influenced by guilt toward our parents and siblings.

Why do we use "mimicking"? What are the reasons behind this behavior? Remember the warning "I hope your children do to you what you've done to me"? You were blamed for your parents' suffering, and they wanted you to suffer the same way at the hands of your children. And so you do. Four reasons explain why.

MIMICKING: PUNISHMENT AND RELIEF

We become like our parents to punish ourselves and relieve our guilt for hurting them. If you think you're responsible for causing your parents' unhappiness, suffering, disappointment, getting out of control, then you deserve to be punished by having the same faults. Huh? Think of it like this, if *you* are unhappy, suffer, are disappointed, or out of control, then *you* have paid yourself back for the suffering you caused them. Think of the biblical expression, "an eye for an eye." This requires that a punishment fit the crime *exactly*. It turns out that your conscience operates the same way. It requires that you be punished *exactly* in the way you've made another person suffer; in this case, your parents or sibling.

When your overprotective parent became frantic with worry when you played sports, you felt responsible for causing their worry. They screamed with anxiety, "You'll break your leg! You'll get killed!" And how does your conscience operate? It requires your becoming frantic with worry when *your* kids are playing, just as your parents did with you. There. Now you've been punished for your long-ago offense of causing your parents to feel frantic with worry over you.

Remember the indigenous tribe described in Chapter 1? Remember how they blamed themselves for earthquakes, floods, volcanic eruptions, and so on? A child blames him- or herself when a parent continually acts badly. Later on in life, being like that parent keeps the grown child from feeling better off than the parent. This is how our conscience evens the score.

If you blame yourself for the explosive rages your domineering, overbearing father suffered when you didn't submit to him, you'd assume that your independent attitude was responsible. You could do penance for your guilt toward him by becoming domineering with others and explosive with your own children. Why is this "penance"? Because by mimicking your father, you also suffer when your children act independently of you.

Does this sound self-destructive? It is. Surely, you'd prefer to not fly off the handle and rail at your children. And just as surely you'd rather not suffer when they don't submit to you. But the idea is that if you caused your parents or siblings to suffer, you deserve to suffer in the same way. It's precisely this idea, the dynamic of self-blame, that's central to why we behave in ways that we hate.

That explains the first of the four reasons why we choose

to suffer through mimicking our parents' behavior. Let's look at the second reason.

MIMICKING: DON'T FEEL BAD— WE'RE IN THIS TOGETHER

If you've ever felt bad because you think it's not fair to be better off than your parents, you might resort to mimicking to relieve your bad feelings. At a talk I gave, a woman told me about her experience with her obese mother. She remembered not only sitting with her during meals and snacks, but she also recalled mimicking her mother's overeating because she thought that would comfort her mother. Her exact words were, "I felt she would feel comforted because we were in it together." What was she really saying? "Don't feel bad, Mom, I have the same [overeating] problem that you have." That's the second reason for mimicking behaviors we hate. What's the third?

MIMICKING: PUSHING AWAY THE PAIN

For the most part, we all want to forget our unpleasant experiences of the past and have the bad feelings associated with them fade away. This done, we can enjoy our present-day lives. Now factor this in: By mistreating others the way we've been mistreated, we help forget that we suffered at the hands of our parents. How does that help, you're probably wondering?

Imagine you've gone through something terrible like childhood abuse. (The victim could have been you or perhaps someone else in the family.) The result is that you can't stand thinking about it, that you want to bury the memory and never reexperience the pain of it again. The farther removed from it you get, in physical distance *and* in time, the safer you feel and the less likely you are to think about it. What helps you accomplish this? Being as far removed as possible from your memories of the traumatic experience. What could be farther away from that opposite position? To become the one who mistreats, not the one is mistreated.

If as an adult you act possessively toward your children, you demand underlying loyalty and overt demonstrations of love the way your parents did with you, it'll help you forget the pain you felt when your parent was that way with you. What pain? Maybe out of loyalty to your possessive parent, you inhibited your relationships with others. Or maybe you cut off new relationships because you feared being trapped by the demands of loyalty you felt all relationships came with. Either way, you suffer. And now, as an adult, if you dominate your children, maybe you'll forget that you yourself submitted to your own domineering parents. You don't want to recall painful memories of having been cheated out of your own independence.

With three reasons for mimicking looked at and understood, we're left with one more. Here's how that one shapes our world of self-blame.

MIMICKING: WORKING HARD TO IMPROVE THE FLAW

By doing to others what was done to you, you hope to meet people who can show you how to better cope with the behavior that harmed you. That's the basic premise, and it's a lot to take in, so let's look at it from another angle. These new people you meet become role models for you in learning new ways of dealing with behavior that was painful or difficult for you in the past. If you think about couples you know, you'll find that this is often true. And if you've ever wondered why many couples have extreme opposite personalities that often clash, you now have the answer to all your wondering. A submissive person, who gives in easily, is with a domineering partner who tends not to. Why? Each one is actually learning from the other how to improve on his or her own shortcoming.

These four reasons are why, in spite of your best intentions, you may have acquired those qualities of your parents that you hated the most. In the case of David, a smart businessman who undermined his career success, you'll see that he did this because of his father and because he identified with some of his father's qualities.

▥ **DAVID** ▥

David was not going to outdo his father. He was a forty-five-year-old businessman who came to me because his job was threatened as a result of his insensitivity to other people's opinions of him. When David's employees or business partners offered suggestions, he would immediately find fault with them. Not only that, he'd (unknowingly) act contemptuous of them, and never miss the chance to pontificate on his own views.

David was totally unaware of this pattern of his, which was causing a great deal of difficulties for him in his business. His partners were becoming more and more critical of him because of the dissention in his division of the company. They were also tired of his insensitivity to *their* constructive criticisms of him, and they warned him that he might be demoted if he didn't correct his attitude. It was that piece of news that brought David in to see me.

At first, David denied that the friction within the firm was his fault. Instead, he insisted that it was his partners' lack of receptivity to his ideas that was the problem. However, over time, David began to acknowledge that there *were* some problems and they did in fact involve disagreements with him. But he also insisted that they would have all been overcome if his ideas for solving them were only acted upon.

How did David's contempt for others come into play when David was interacting with me? Actually, his contempt for me was quite evident when we worked together. Often, he diminished the value of my comments and sometimes he'd say that he forgot what I had said to him during the previous session. Occasionally, David would flat out tell me that my ideas were wrong, then present his own explanations, which, he said, "were more to the point."

Instead of acting defensively, or getting angry, I usually asked him to tell me more about his criticisms of me and how it felt to dismiss what I had to say. Sometimes David was relieved and said that he was surprised that I wasn't critical of him for dismissing his ideas. At other times he told me that he felt uncomfortable criticizing me. Asked about this, he said that he was concerned about hurting my feelings. After we had a number of these exchanges, David started to soften his tone. Soon he began to tell me about his father.

David's father had done poorly as a mid-level manager in a mid-sized medical supply company; his abrasive personally had a lot to do with his lack of success, and eventually he was forced out. From then on, he managed to earn a modest living as a consultant. His explanation for why he left the firm was that his ideas weren't taken seriously because of bureaucratic infighting. Throughout David's childhood, and until his father's death four years before David starting seeing me, his father had always been contemptuous of David's opinions. He'd tell David, in a variety of ways, that they were worthless. This was always followed by a long-winded lecture during which David's father would pontificate and boast about his knowledge and experience.

How did David process this life-long pattern? He took it to mean that his father was insecure and easily threatened if he wasn't right. He also assumed that his own intelligence posed a threat to his father's self-esteem. And so, in order to not threaten his father, David *accommodated* him by presenting opinions that were weak or silly. He did this in order to provide his father with the opportunity to criticize him and act superior. Obviously, David didn't behave this way with his partners; instead he treated *them* the way his dad treated *him*.

The more success David had in his business career, the guiltier he felt toward his father. Knowing with certainty that his father had to be on top, subconsciously David worried that his father would feel outdone and insecure. In order to *not* be superior to him, David mimicked him. (Again, this was done on a subconscious level.) He behaved in the same counterproductive way toward others as his dad behaved toward him, and he achieved the same negative results. Acting this way toward others also helped David to keep memories of his childhood humiliations at the hands of his father out of his conscious awareness.

How did David gain access to the beginnings of his self-destructive behavior (for example, the memories of his negative childhood experiences with his father and their impact on his life)? Remember that he often acted contemptuous of my ideas and me in the same way his father acted toward him? Because I didn't act hurt or defensive (the way David had felt when this had been done to him), I provided a model of how to face what had been painful for him so that he could remember and see how his behavior had developed in relation to his father. The less guilty he felt toward his father, the easier it became for David to be less scornful and more receptive to his business partners. ▪

Accommodation, Rebellion, and Mimicking: Working You Over

Most people are affected by *one* of the three mechanisms: accommodation, rebellion, or mimicking. But when *all three* exist in a single person, it may be much more difficult to understand the problem. Perhaps you find that you accommodate, rebel, and mimic at various times in your relationships.

Maybe you *accommodate* the possessive parent by remaining overly devoted to him or her. But in your relationship with others to whom you may also feel obligated to be extremely devoted, at times you *rebel*. You do this by avoiding people who want you to be close to them. And later in life, when you have children of your own, you *mimic* your parent by being possessive of your own children and jealous of their interest in others. Yet mainly, people perceive you as a person who is overly devoted to others. Tina is an example of this.

▪ TINA ▪

Tina was pulled by her mother's needs. She was a teenager with a severe drinking problem that caused problems for her in school and with her friends. Though she had no idea at the time, Tina eventually came to understand that her behavior stemmed from the fact that she grew up under an overly possessive mother. And so, Tina's behavior was classic rebellion.

It started in Tina's early childhood. Even back then, Tina's mother acted very needy and had to be involved in all parts of her daughter's life. When Tina showed interest in her father, her mother was unhappy. The same held true when Tina was interested in her friends. Not surprisingly, Tina had a hard time separating from her mother, beginning in preschool. At that time, Tina was unhappy in school. She cried and wanted to come home, but it wasn't that she missed and needed her mother; it was that *her mother missed and needed her.* As Tina got older, her mother continued to hold on to her, causing Tina to feel angry and frustrated. Tina believed her mother didn't want her to have fun; she just wanted Tina to focus all her attention on her. And when Tina did have fun, she saw that it hurt her mother; she knew her mother felt rejected and guilt set in. And so, in order for her to have fun, Tina had to drink. When she was drunk she felt less inhibited about partying and having sex with boys. This behavior upset her mother, who didn't understand that it was a rebellion against her overpossessiveness.

Gradually, Tina began realizing what was motivating her excessive drinking (and promiscuous behavior) and gradually she began to gain control over it. She realized she'd been limiting her friendships with others out of *accommodation* to her possessive mother, and had been drinking to *rebel* against it. She was fortunate to have solved her problem early, before it became too self-destructive.

Summing It Up

Born with no previous experiences in life, children tend to blame themselves for the worst flaws of their parents and siblings. By blaming themselves and changing their normal behavior, they hope to end the parent/sibling behaviors that are detrimental and painful. The ways they choose among are to accommodate, rebel against, and/or mimic their parents' worst flaws.

Exercises: Now Look at Yourself

How do you cope? Which are you? An accommodator? A rebel? A mimic? If you think you're an accommodator, ask yourself, is the behavior you don't like in yourself a result of trying to not hurt or threaten anyone in your family or others currently in your life? If you think you're a rebel, ask yourself, is your problem behavior a response to refusing to go along with what your parents expected of you? Or ask yourself, are you behaving in ways opposite to what you know others in your life want? If you think you're a mimic, ask yourself, is the behavior you don't like in yourself similar to anyone in your family? Or ask yourself, did anyone act that way toward you?

Read the short scenarios that follow with those questions in mind. Figuring out your response will help you start to see more about yourself.

Scenario 1

I was at a business meeting today and the head of my department stood up and congratulated us on getting a major client of ours to renew their contract. He asked us to talk about the contribution each of us made. When it came time to me, I . . .

- Didn't highlight my design work and instead deferred to my co-worker Nancy, letting her take the credit. (That night I was furious at myself for not taking the recognition I knew I deserved.)

- Cracked some sly jokes about our company's practice of self-congratulatory back-patting and passed off to the next person. (That night I felt like a jerk, wondering, "what was that about?")

- Subtly put down a co-worker's contribution while punching up mine. (That night I wanted to kick myself when I remembered all the times my dad did that to me.)

Not sure of your response? Let's look at another scenario.

Scenario 2

I was at home tonight, making dinner for the family. My daughter came in and asked if we could go outside and shoot some baskets. I said:

- "Okay," knowing it would push back the work I brought home from the office and I'd be up later than I wanted— I've sworn I'd start getting more sleep.

- "No!" immediately, before the sentence was even out of her mouth and even though it would really not affect me one way or the other.

- "Oh, I'm so tired from work, I worked so hard, how can you ask me such a thing knowing how much I do all day, every single day and knowing it's just so *much* for me, so *stressful* for me, so *hard* for me?" I find a reason to reject a reasonable request just as my parents did when as a kid I made a reasonable request

Moving Ahead

These scenarios are designed to get you to start looking a little more closely at your responses in life; they're here to help you see how the three mechanisms (accommodation, rebellion, and mimicking) enter your life like uninvited dinner guests. Let's see how they found their way to your door in the first place.

CHAPTER 5

Is Blaming Your Parents Justified?

1. Parents aren't perfect.
2. They don't have to be.
3. All families have problems.

Sometimes those three statements shock us. But often what's even more shocking to us is that by understanding *how* we were negatively affected by our family's problems (and their effects continue into our adult lives), we can use that information to change. What's also shocking to many is that change—true change, long-lasting change— is really an option. It is.

May the Force Be with Us?
Let's Hope So

Inside all of us is an inborn force pushing us to develop our talents, propelling us to become as strong as possible. We need this force. It helps us leave our nest; it spurs us on to become successful. Because this force beats so powerfully in us, there's no good reason to limit ourselves and not achieve life's possibilities.

But actually there *is* a reason. It's a parent or sibling whose extreme behaviors persist for a long period of time. When that's present, children develop destructive patterns, and they can often last throughout adulthood.

What Are the Arguments?

"My father was an alcoholic." "My mother ran around with other men." "I was poor." "I was neglected." Isn't that sad? Don't you feel sorry for me? *Please pay attention to me.* Does this sound familiar? If so, you may know someone who uses this victim perspective to get through his or her life. Or perhaps it sounds familiar because you yourself are that person, the one playing the role of victim to your parents' role of victimizer.

Some people say that criticizing parents isn't justified. They also say that the people who *do* criticize their parents or siblings have exaggerated fantasies about their childhood suffering. They say it's done as a way to get attention or sympathy or to avoid responsibility. And finally, they say a person who criticizes his or her parents is an ungrateful, spoiled, child who never grew up. The Bible instructs us, "Honor thy father and thy mother." And a person who does anything less is worthy of contempt. People argue that the past isn't important. All that's needed for us to change, they say, is that we *focus* on changing our behavior—that we be strong, use willpower, follow someone else's positive example, and think positively. If we adhere to these things, life will improve. And if it doesn't? Well, it's probably our own fault because we weren't doing enough to make the change happen.

If you really thought about it, would any of that make any sense? No. And now, welcome back to reality.

Do you honestly know anyone who *doesn't* want to be happy? How about successful? Fulfilled? Yes, there are people who act like victims to get attention or perhaps to avoid acting responsibly. And yes, they're doing it in response to damaging family experiences of the past. But think about this: Why should a suffering child cease to feel pain because he or she's become an adult?

Effective or Ineffective?

Certain behaviors are annoying. It's a simple truth that whining to get attention is annoying. So is complaining to avoid responsibility. And clearly, these behaviors are *not effective*. So, the question here is, *why would a person go out of his or her way to get attention and avoid responsibility by being ineffective and by annoying people?* Given the choice, they wouldn't. But here's the twist—*they weren't given the choice.* They're victims of a past they had no control over, and they continue to be victims in the present. *When children experience mistreatment, they blame themselves and suffer. They suffer as children* and *they suffer as adults.*

Hidden from Your Consciousness, but They're Just the Same

We're talking about your self-defeating motivations here—and they *are* here. It's just that they're lurking beneath your conscious awareness and so you don't know what they're doing, what havoc they're wreaking in your life. *What* "havoc?" you're thinking. Your self-destructive behaviors. Your whining, your complaining, your stubbornness, your shirking of responsibilities. And there's a very good reason for these behaviors, self-destructive though they may be; it's called *relief.*

We get relief when we escape the guilt brought on by our parents' or siblings' harmful behavior. What's another way to describe this form of relief? How about *self-defeating motivation?* There are two major types. Remember *accommodation* and *rebellion* from Chapter 4? Well, they're back, but this time playing different roles in our lives. To recap accommodation, it's a dance between parent and child: A parent acts wounded by the child's behavior, and the child is motivated to accommodate (even if it means behaving in ways that go against his or her best interests). The reason for the child's motivation? To *not* feel guilty about wounding his or her parent and to preserve their relationship.

Remember David from Chapter 4? David's father criticized and dismissed his son's ideas because he was insecure. David *felt guilty* about showing his own intelligence because it hurt and threatened his father. David was *motivated* to *not feel guilty* about hurting his father, and so he presented weak and silly ideas to his father. His father criticized him and felt superior to David, David's guilt was relieved, his relationship with his father was preserved: Mission accomplished.

An important point: Accommodation itself—the act of saying "yes" to please another person—is a normal behavior. It's necessary in order to get along with others and make your way in the world. Only when accommodation becomes *excessive* does it lead to self-defeating outcomes.

And now to the second type of relief that shows up in the form of self-defeating motivations—*rebellion*. A brief recap reminds us that this is caused by the child's struggle or *rebellion* against a parent's excessive expectations. Why rebel? The reasons are actually very sound: to promote our own goals, or to communicate a protest against the offending behavior that we'd like to stop. We haven't met Meg. Meg's story will help us better understand rebellion, in the context of self-defeating motivations.

▦   MEG   ▦

Meg was rebelling against authority. She was difficult, and her mother was an excessive, sometimes cruel disciplinarian. Instead of being compliant and doing whatever her mother wanted, Meg went in the absolute opposite direction: She did *nothing* her mother wanted and went out of her way to do what she knew her mother *didn't* want her to do. At her wit's end with Meg and becoming more and more frustrated, she dished out corporal punishment almost daily, but still failed to change her daughter's behavior. And what about Meg? What was her response to her mother's strict discipline? In addition to being stubborn and habitually late, she was hostile toward anyone in a position of authority, she dressed provocatively, she behaved promiscuously, too. Another word to describe Meg's behavior? Rebellion.

Like accommodation, rebellion in itself is a normal behavior, and it's necessary to promote self-interest. Rebellion is also a form of communication. It allows kids, like Meg, the chance to show their parents that the parents' behavior is unacceptable. Only when rebellion, like accommodation, becomes excessive does it lead to self-defeating outcomes. ■

Hide and Seek

It's probably becoming clear that recognizing self-defeating motivations is an important part of overcoming your limitations and achieving your life's goals. Yet it's hard to recognize things that almost always remain hidden from your conscious awareness. It's just as hard to solve any problem unless you can see its cause. And many people, in spite of their own obvious personal difficulties, have trouble accepting that the cause of their current problems lies in problems they experienced in their families.

But how can you be sure that your parents' flaws are responsible for *your problems?* And if your self-defeating motivations remain hidden, how do you know that they even exist? Two tricky questions to be sure, but both have a fairly simple response. We know by observing the *results* of the flawed behavior you exhibit: your self-defeating patterns.

Some people like to cite genetics as the basis for the problems I've been describing here. Genetics *is* responsible for many inborn personality qualities, such as being intelligent, aggressive, outgoing, reserved, and the like. But if genetics was the sole cause of all of our problems, how can we explain why a very bright child might do extremely well in school and go on to become a perennial student with many degrees, but be unable to successfully hold down a job, advance in his career, or manage his investments? Is there a specific money-making gene? How about one for holding a job? What do you think?

Remembering Their Faults, Forgetting Why You're Unhappy

That's enough about genetics. Let's start looking at how a parent's behavior creates the environment that either hinders or promotes the child's development. Sometimes people may actually recall specific problems of their family members, yet still have no idea how the problems are connected to their current difficulties. Dr. Joe was just like that.

▓ DR. JOE ▓

Dr. Joe was punishing himself. He was a successful doctor, practicing medicine for twenty years with a loyal patient clientele. Despite all the success and support and loyalty, Dr. Joe was always anxious. He feared losing his license and going to jail, and though he suffered greatly (and constantly) from this anxiety, he had no idea what its cause was.

During our first session, Dr. Joe began telling me that his mother had always demanded flawless schoolwork, nothing less than perfection in everything he did. This demand for perfection was reinforced by strict Catholic teachings, which his mother supported. On confession days, Joe searched his conscience for every possible sinful thought to confess, or else he feared he would burn in hell. He never understood why his angst about this was so much more intense than many of his Catholic friends felt. They used to make jokes about their church's many religious requirements or say things like "just decide which sins are okay to keep and which ones don't count." But Joe couldn't do that. His obsessive preoccupation with the church's rules and regulations didn't let him.

Our first session ended with us talking about Dr. Joe's motivation for his severe anxiety and his fear of disappointing his mother's unrealistic expectations of him. To disappoint his mother, a woman who demanded perfection, was his greatest sin, and his exaggerated fears of severe punishment (that is, losing his license and being sent to prison) reflected how guilty he felt about the slightest mistake.

The following week, Dr. Joe came in and spoke about his father. He described him as a worried, unhappy man, a college dropout who was always putting down his (Dr. Joe's) accomplishments at school. Dr. Joe grew up hearing things like, "You think you're so good at school, but wait until you get into the business world, you'll see how tough life really is." When I asked Dr. Joe how that affected him, he said, "I could easily outdo him, but I was afraid of making him feel bad and proving him wrong because he already felt bad about himself. I thought that he was jealous of me."

I explained to him that the other reason for his punishment worries was the need to relieve his guilt about outshining his father by being a successful doctor. Dr. Joe's immediate thought was, "If I worry about lawsuits, it proves to my father that I'm not the big star. I completely discount that 99 percent of my patients love me. I only highlight the rare person who is unhappy with me."

In the third session, it occurred to Dr. Joe why he'd been unable to recognize his father's negative impact on him. "I feel bad for thinking that his jealousy of my success caused me so many problems, and I don't want to hurt him *again* by thinking bad things about him. He didn't have the best life."

By the fifth session Dr. Joe could appreciate that while he was pleasing his mother with his accomplishments in school and career, he was antagonizing his father. And by limiting himself to appease his father, he was disappointing his mother. As intelligent and educated as Dr. Joe was, and in spite of having a clear-eyed view of his parents' faults, Dr. Joe was totally unaware of his self-defeating motivations. However, once he became aware of the connection between his relationship with his parents and his punishment thoughts, his anxiety about terrible things happening to him began lessening. As he began consciously applying his understanding to his irrational reactions, things began to get better for Dr. Joe. He reported that for the first time in his life, he was beginning to feel relaxed and to have fun. He'd gotten significant control over his guilt feelings toward his parents, and his self-inflicted requirements for punishment began to disappear.

Denial, Your Parents, and Rose-Colored Glasses

Denying the difficulties of your past and choosing instead to look at it all through rose-colored glasses is a natural thing. No one likes to have painful experiences or remember such experiences. Being able to see your troubled family experiences clearly means reexperiencing your parents' and siblings' shortcomings and the lifelong problems they have caused you. *But you still need to take off the glasses.* However, you *also* need to understand that if you do take them off, the world will eventually be rosier without them.

For Dr. Joe, taking off his rose-colored glasses meant remembering the painful, relentless demands made on him by his mother and being back in touch with his father's depression and jealousy of him. It also brought back the anger and anxiety he dealt with for years because of both parents. But accepting that he needed to experience the pain if he ever wanted to relieve himself of it altogether made Dr. Joe go forward.

How Do You Spell Relief?

People want to relieve their pain, and one way to find relief is to *mimic* the offending parent. When you are the perpetrator, it helps distance you from remembering when you were the victim. Mimicking is not only a common method of denial; it's also very effective.

Who's Grading the Parents? Whitewashing, Part I

Denial is sneaky. It shows up in unexpected ways, such as when you give your parents or siblings better grades than they deserve in order to keep you from seeing their flaws (which caused you unhappiness). The more obscure the truth is, the more you can forget. The more you forget, the easier it is to not reexperience your feelings of guilt and resentment, the accommodation, rebellion, and mimicking behaviors that have spoiled your life. You might deceive yourself into thinking of your parents' authoritarian behavior as strength, that their overly possessive attitudes really were caring, and their rejection was really about character building. And you might persuade yourself that living through your accomplishments was supportive and admiring, not needy and weak. *Consciously,* you delude yourself, but *unconsciously,* you perceive your parents' personalities correctly.

The Denial Continues: Whitewashing, Part II

Not only do you fail to see the harmful qualities in your parents, but you also fail to see the qualities in *yourself* that you can't stand.

Have you ever found yourself strongly disliking a specific quality in someone else? It's often because that one quality is the same quality you can't stand in yourself, but have hidden from your awareness. It's very unpleasant to recognize that you give in to others too much, or that you refuse to go along with requests, that you're too self-centered, critical, rejecting, insensitive, controlling, and so on. So, in order to *not* recognize your own flaws (which make you feel disappointed or disgusted with yourself), you direct your contempt toward whoever else possesses those qualities. This is exactly what Beth did.

▓ BETH ▓

Beth was not a "kiss up." She couldn't stand a complimentary co-worker who, she said, "kissed up" to his superiors and anyone else who "had something he wanted." Her dislike bordered on obsession. Yet, over time it became apparent that Beth had a similar appeasing, kissing-up quality that she'd kept hidden from her awareness. When she started digging around deep inside, Beth began to understand more and more about herself and where her extreme reaction to her co-worker was coming from.

Beth started talking more about her parents, and how they stayed together throughout her childhood but how they were alienated and slept in different bedrooms. Days went by when they hardly said a word to one another. As an only child, she was their major source of pleasure, and Beth grew to feel responsible for reassuring each parent (appeasing/accommodating). As an adult, when Beth saw her co-worker behaving in ways in which she had behaved towards her parents as a child, her unhappy childhood memories came flooding back in. At the time, however, she didn't recognize the same behavior in herself. That came a little later, after Beth was more ready to move away from denial.

Knowing the Truth All Along

Like the new car you may be interested in buying, all of us come equipped with certain standard parts. One of them is our ability to know, even unconsciously, whether our parent or sibling is reacting to us from a position of strength or of weakness. Although we may gloss over a lot of their bad behaviors to spare ourselves pain, *unconsciously* we still perceive them correctly. This is because it's too important to our development *not* to perceive our experiences with our parents or siblings correctly. Does that seem like a contradiction? It's not. Think about the ostrich when it buries its head in the sand to be spared seeing danger. Does it mean that danger has been avoided? No. Think about the soldier who puts terrible, bloody war experiences out of his memory. Does it mean that he's avoided being deeply affected by his war experiences for the rest of his life? No.

No matter what you consciously think, no matter how much you have denied, no matter how favorably you view your parents, chances are good that unconsciously you're still able to perceive them, and your siblings, correctly. The result of this correct view? You'll rarely mistake bluster, authority, and self-centeredness for strength. You'd be unlikely to perceive their possessiveness, overprotectiveness, and living through your accomplishments as true interest and concern for you. With you, depression and neediness won't be misperceived for kindness and sensitivity, and you'd be unlikely to believe that emotional coldness and rejection are signs of character and self-discipline.

Therefore, your responses (of accommodation, rebellion, self-blame) are the result of *real* flaws and mistreatments by your parents. You didn't imagine any of it. However, it all still remains hidden, as does the relief from them until you unlock the unconscious conflicts and bring them into your conscious life. Dr. Joe did this, and after he did, he moved forward with his life—a healthier and happier life.

Access to our unconscious is possible. One way of getting to this knowledge is for a sympathetic and understanding person to serve as your ally in exposing the truth. For example, a client, John, had an uncle who brought up certain truths about John's father, which made it possible for John to get in touch with hidden truths about his painful childhood experiences with his abusive father.

A second way of accessing self-knowledge is through your negative reaction to people who have the qualities in yourself or in your family members that you can't stand. Like Beth in her reaction to her co-worker, your own negative reactions show that you are still in touch with your past painful experiences, even though you do not consciously recognize it.

Exercise: Now Look at Yourself

Which Animal Are You?

We talked about how the ostrich sticks its head in the sand. Now it's time for you to take a look at yourself and figure out which animal you are. Don't see yourself on the list? There are a lot of animals out there that aren't on the list. M aybe you'll come up with one (or some) on your own.

Are you an ostrich? Trouble is there, I don't want to see it.

Are you a bull? Trouble is there, I'll charge in and destroy it.

Are you a chameleon? Trouble is there, I'll change myself to fit in and avoid it.

Are you a turtle? Trouble is there, I'll protect myself.

Are you a fox? Trouble is there, I'll sneak around and see what happens.

Are you another animal? Which one? How do you react to trouble?

Moving Ahead

How can we recognize those things we keep tightly (and safely) stowed away from our view in our unconscious? Therapy is not for everyone, and radio shrinks aren't either. What then? A simple method of self-understanding through charts that are easy to use can help. Read on.

CHAPTER 6

Charts: Looking at Yourself in the Mirror and Seeing Your Family

Earlier I said that if you wanted to be more beautiful but you lived in a world without mirrors it would be hard for you to know whether you needed to improve your hair, your complexion, your teeth, or some other part of your body. Think of the charts in this chapter as your mirror, quickly showing you what's holding you back from achieving your goals.

Now that you understand how the mechanisms of accommodation, rebellion, and mimicking affect your life, these charts will help you see how you can start applying what you understand in a general way to yourself in a very specific way. These charts are your light, illuminating your hidden self-defeating motivations.

Using the Charts

To understand how to best use these charts, take a look at the first one below: "What Happened to You When Your Parents and Siblings Acted Badly." This chart will give you an overview of how people get stuck in so many ways.

First, scan down the far left column and find the flaw or failing that is closest to your parents' or siblings'. After finding it, move across the top row of the columns to see how you responded (that is, accommodating, rebelling, mimicking). Finally, read down each column to see how your behavior shows up in your life. For instance, where your response to a *controlling and authoritarian* parent could have led you to *accommodate* by becoming overly respectful of authority or to *rebel* by acting stubborn, contrary, or defiant. If you *mimicked* your parent, you would have become demanding and controlling toward your children and others. It is also possible that all three responses (accommodation, rebellion, and mimicking) show up in your behaviors.

Continue down the far left column and locate the other parental weaknesses and defects and check out the different self-defeating responses to them.

Summing Up

Now you've seen, clearly and logically, how your parents' and siblings' shortcomings affect you today. Okay, now what? The next chart shows you how you created new rules to live by so you could survive in the environment you called home. This second chart will shine more light on why you are who you are. Self-knowledge is a process, but at least now you have started your process, and help, in the form of change, will soon be on the way.

Thou Shall Not . . .

How do you feel when you break one of the ten moral rules better known as the Ten Commandments? Or, for that matter, breaking any other set of ethical rules that govern other religions? Most likely you feel guilt. Sometimes you even feel queasy just *thinking* of breaking one.

Sometimes your sense of guilt for possibly committing a sin automatically keeps you on the correct path. For instance, Commandment #8, "Thou Shall Not Steal," is fixed in your *unconscious* mind and automatically governs your behavior. You don't have to go through the process of thinking that

WHAT HAPPENED TO YOU WHEN YOUR PARENTS AND SIBLINGS ACTED BADLY

Your Parents' or Siblings' Flaw	When You Accommodate	When You Rebel and Protest	When You Mimic, and Do to Others What Was Done to You
Excessively controlling and authoritarian	You overrespect authority, are submissive, and excessively obedient.	You are stubborn, defiant, and contrary.	You are bossy, demanding and expect obedience to you and the rules.
Weak and ineffectual	You have to be strong, take charge, and be in control.	You ignore others' problems and let them flounder.	You are meek and give in to what others want.
Possessive	You are overly loyal, and afraid to be separate.	You reject demands and keep your distance from those who want you to be close to them.	You suffocate others, and feel easily jealous of attention paid to others, even violently.
Rejecting	You are self-reliant, don't show your feelings, and avoid close relationships.	You demand attention and act destructively, if necessary.	You are indifferent to others and enjoy seeing them hurt.
Overprotective	You are very cautious about doing sports and physical activities.	You are careless, reckless, and a daredevil type.	You see danger everywhere, and restrict your kids.

Your Parents' or Siblings' Flaw	When You Accommodate	When You Rebel and Protest	When You Mimic, and Do to Others What Was Done to You
Underprotective	You take chances and don't notice the usual signs of danger.	You are too cautious and overly alert to danger.	You ignore signs of danger, especially with your children.
Competitive and self-centered	You are afraid to speak up or stand out. You limit your successes with looks, or career, or parenting.	You avoid giving credit and go out of your way to get attention.	You put down others, enjoy their faults, and need to be the center of attention.
Self-effacing and modest	You are uncomfortable highlighting your virtues.	You become boastful, and enjoy taking center stage.	You are self-effacing.
Critical	You have low self-esteem, accept blame easily, and may feel "why try?"	You deny anything is ever your fault	You are quick to blame others even when they have done no wrong.
Live through your accomplishments	You have to be perfect, and stand out. You are anxious about failing.	You hide your accomplishments, and may deliberately fail.	You expect perfection and are too critical of mistakes.

Overly righteous and disdainful	You highlight your moral failings and may run afoul of the law.	You parade your moral virtues.	You are disdainful of others and highlight their moral flaws.
Amoral	You have trouble following the rules.	You insist on honesty in all your dealings and don't tolerate cheats.	You use people and use any means to get what you want.
Depressed	You feel guilty about being happy. You have to help others in order to feel good.	You are insensitive to and avoid unhappy people.	You complain all the time. No one can make you happy. You always look grim.
Abuse drugs and alcohol	You become very vigilant and try to avoid setting them off. You feel unprotected and have to be the parent.	You hate anyone not in control.	You are unpredictable and explosive. You are attracted to drugs and alcohol.
Abusive	You feel irrationally at fault. You do anything to please.	You fight back as much as possible. You go through life angry, have a chip on your shoulder.	You become a bully and physically abuse others the way you were treated.

the act of stealing is wrong because "my father said so, and my minister taught me about it," any more than you go through a thinking process when you have a close call on the freeway. In that situation you don't think to yourself "there is danger ahead and I need to steer to the left and then brake hard, and then accelerate." Instead, you automatically and reflexively do what will work to save your life.

Religious beliefs aren't the only rules that are set in your mind and that, if ignored, will make you feel guilty. The beliefs you have that are based on your dealings with your flawed parents and siblings will also create guilt in you if you break them.

What are some of these personal beliefs? One might be "Loyalty is best." This would have been learned if every day you had to deal with an overpossessive parent. "Obedience is best" is another personal belief that could have been learned from dealing with your authoritarian parent. Though such rules can cause you to act self-destructively, you'll still feel guilty if you ignore them. The result? They have the exact same power over your behavior as the religious rules you learned as a child, for example, stealing is wrong.

"How You Create New Moral Rules to Live By" charts how your experiences with your parents and siblings lead to the development of many of these rules for living. These new moral beliefs automatically determine many of the behaviors that you dislike in yourself. For example, your experience with an authoritarian parent has taught you that he or she is hurt when you act independently and think for yourself. In order to relieve your guilt about causing hurt by disobeying, you'll develop your own automatic moral rule to live by—"Obedience is best."

As in the preceding chart, once you identify your parent/sibling behavior, read across to see if the moral rules are rules that look familiar to ones that *you* created to cope in your family situation.

HOW YOU CREATE NEW MORAL RULES TO LIVE BY

When Your Parent or Sibling Is	They Are Hurt and Disturbed When You	Your Thoughts That Please Them Are	Your New Moral Command (Rule) Is
Excessively controlling and authoritarian.	Act independently and defy their authority.	"It is best to follow their rules and do what I am told."	Obedience is best.
Depressed and needy.	Don't sacrifice for them, take care of them, or feel sorry for them.	"It is wrong to focus on making myself happy."	Saving and rescuing the downtrodden is good.
Possessive and need you to be involved with them.	Are involved with, or think highly of others.	"It is wrong to be separate or to value others highly."	Loyalty is best.
Rejecting when you want to be close to and dependent on them.	Want to be close or have your needs met.	"It is wrong to be close, intimate, or dependent."	Independence is best.
Self-centered and competitive with you.	Try to be noticed, admired, or successful.	"It is wrong to stand out or to be accomplished."	Modesty and restraint are best. Don't outshine others.
Failing financially or with career or school.	Are doing well.	"It is wrong to succeed or outdo them."	Don't outshine others.
Live through your accomplishments.	Fail to succeed or stand out.	"It is wrong to fail, make mistakes, and not be perfect."	Success is everything. The means justify the ends.
Use drugs and are unpredictable.	Confront them and demand reliability.	"Don't make demands or expect parenting."	Self-reliance and control are best.

HOW YOU CREATE NEW MORAL RULES TO LIVE BY (continued)

When Your Parent or Sibling Is	They Are Hurt and Disturbed When You	Your Thoughts That Please Them Are	Your New Moral Command (Rule) Is
Overly critical.	Refuse to accept blame.	"I'm at fault no matter what the criticism."	Never be above criticism.
Overprotective.	Take chances or are reckless.	"It is wrong to be adventurous."	Caution is best.
Underprotective.	Are watchful and cautious.	"It is wrong to be cautious."	Risk and adventure are good.
Amoral.	Do what is right and honest.	"It is wrong to be moral."	Dishonesty is best. Get what you want, no matter how.
Self-righteous and disdainful of others.	Don't follow the straight and narrow.	"It is wrong to disobey the rules."	Righteousness above all.

Governed by the Thoughts You Hate

In addition to these moral rules, which can govern your life, you may be plagued by thoughts about yourself that you can't stand. "I'm a lazy bum," "Who do I think I am?," "I'm stubborn as a mule," "I'm just a baby." In the next chart you can see how your parent's flaws led to these thoughts, thoughts that you can't stand, which you may be unable to get out of your mind.

Do you feel as if a devil, ghost, or other such outside force has taken over your mind and infected it with ideas that you hate? Ideas that directly conflict with the values you would rather hold? The next chart, "How Your Parents' Behavior Can Lead to Thoughts That Plague You," will help you start to see how those ideas came to reside in your mind. This is the first step to being able to clear your mind of them.

Samantha was a woman who was plagued by thoughts that made her life miserable.

▦   SAMANTHA   ▦

Samantha was at war with herself. "I'm a compulsive nut and a nervous wreck," are the words she used to describe herself. When trying to relax, sleep late, read a magazine, or take a nap, she became tortured by thoughts such as "Get out of bed, you lazy bitch," "What the hell is wrong with you?," "How could you be so selfish?," "Wash the goddamned dishes," and "Get your ass in gear." Samantha was torn: Every time she wanted to do something for herself, she couldn't because she felt required to obey her thoughts about taking care of chores and responsibilities. And when she tried to ignore these commands, the thoughts increased in intensity and she became very anxious.

HOW YOUR PARENTS' BEHAVIOR CAN LEAD TO THOUGHTS THAT PLAGUE YOU

When Your Parents or Siblings Are Excessively	When You Accommodate, You Think	When You Feel Guilty for Rebelling, You Accept Their Criticisms of You	When You Act Like Them, You Think
Controlling and authoritarian	"Obedience is good." "Respect your elders." "Parents know best." "God and country above all."	"I'm just as stubborn as a mule." "I'd better get my ass in gear and stop being so lazy."	"Do what I say." "Follow the rules." "You think you know it all."
Rejecting	"Self-reliance is best." "Showing feelings is weakness." "Don't depend on others."	"I'm too needy." "I'm too emotional." "I'm just a baby."	"Don't bother me." "Keep your feelings to yourself." "I'm too busy."
Possessive	"Loyalty is best." "Stay away from strangers." "Blood is thicker than water."	"I'm just a flirt." "I'm a traitor." "I don't think of anyone but myself."	"How come you never call or write?" "After all I have done for you." "No one is good enough for you."
Overprotective	"Caution is good." "The world is a dangerous place." "I could easily get hurt or killed."	"I'm so careless." "I never watch where I'm going." "I throw caution to the wind."	"You're going to kill yourself." "Watch your step." "Where are you going?"

Competitive and self-centered	"Modesty is good." "Don't be seen, don't be heard." "The meek shall inherit the earth."	"I'm a smart ass." "I'm a show off." "Who do I think I am?" "I'm stupid, ugly, and phony."	"I know best." "I'm great." "Look how stupid and disgusting they are." "You think you know it all."
Depressed and needy	"Compassion is best." "Save the poor and downtrodden." "What can I do to help?"	"I'm too sensitive." "I'm too selfish and don't think of others."	"Woe is me." "Everything is terrible." "Life is such a burden." "What's the point of living?"
Living through your accomplishments	"Perfection is best." "Succeed at all costs." "My job is never done." "I'll never fail."	"I can't do anything right." "I'm a bum." "I'm a disappointment."	"It's not good enough." "Why can't you get all A's?" "Don't you have more pride?"
Using drugs or alcohol or being unpredictable	"Vigilance is best." "Never let down your guard." "I better watch my step."	"I'm too blasé." "I have my head in the sand." "I don't know what's going on."	"Life is one big party." "Who cares? Live for the moment."

Describing herself as miserable, Samantha was constantly "running around like a chicken with its head cut off," always busy taking care of whatever her children or her husband needed: appointments, social engagements, bills, car repairs, and on and on. Is this different from the way most adults live their lives? You bet it is, because most adults know how to mix business with pleasure and work with play. In other words, they know how to find the balance between doing for others and doing for themselves.

Samantha had no idea how she got this way; she didn't, for example, remember her parents bossing her around, or forcing her to do chores. Digging deeper, however, Samantha described her mother as controlling and demanding. When she didn't get her way, she became cold and rejecting. These qualities contributed to Samantha's problems.

Samantha responded to her mother's controlling and demanding behavior by growing up believing that the way to be liked by her mother was to take care of the household chores (and whatever other needs her mother expressed). When Samantha acted independently of her mother's demands, her mother would act hurt and become cold and rejecting. That caused Samantha to become the compulsively responsible person she is. Samanatha's guilt was the source of the negative thoughts and self-talk that cluttered her mind and made her life one of misery.

Moving Ahead

As mentioned earlier, all the charts and the work you've done in this chapter serve as the exercise and so you'll find no formal "Now Look at Yourself" exercise here. So let's look forward to Part II, where we further investigate the mind-sets that we've uncovered in Part I of this book and really begin to understand them and work through them. By doing this in Part II we'll also start mastering the same mindsets that have previous mastered us.

PART II

WHY IT'S HARD TO END YOUR SUFFERING AND WHAT YOU CAN DO ABOUT IT

CHAPTER 7

Your Family Was Flawed: Why You Can't See the Damage

IF YOU CAN FIGURE OUT how to achieve your goals in many areas of your life, why are problems in other areas so resistant to change? If you know you're highly motivated to change, then why can't you stop behaving in ways that you hate? You're probably beginning to understand that your negative rules for living are buried below the surface of your unconscious mind. They remain hidden from view because of the pain they bring when they rise to the surface. You also know that guilt and resentment contribute to and reinforce your self-defeating behaviors, and you've begun to see how certain behaviors in your family may have been responsible. Yet even though all of this has become obvious, your will power is still not working, so there has to be more.

You may know that your childhood was terrible, but that doesn't mean you can figure out how it causes you pain in your adult life. Read on. What you'll find are some powerful examples of why people may be unable to apply their will-power even when they know that serious problems existed in their families.

Remembering the Drinking, Not the Rescuing

You easily remember your mother or father's alcoholism, but not how it caused you to develop a specific limitation or behavior that you hate today. For example, although you remember having to save your parent from an alcoholic stupor on a regular basis, you might not see how that influenced you to become a rescuer of others today, and often at the expense of taking care of your own needs.

If your intoxicated parent became out of control or possibly even violent when you complained or challenged him or her, you may be unaware that today this is the reason that you're inhibited from speaking out or confronting people about what you dislike. Even if you *do* make the connection between the two, you still may not understand why you have difficulty speaking out with other people, not just with the parent who acted out of control. It may be painful for you to dig down and touch the blame that you felt for causing someone else's out-of-control behavior, but it's your guilt that's still exerting influence over you today and holding you back.

And what if you're struggling with your own drinking problem? You might make the connection between your alcoholism and your parent's. However, you don't understand what compels you to start drinking again after you've become sober. If you blame yourself for a parent's drinking, you won't feel you deserve any better for yourself. Even after you've become sober, your self-blame will cause you to start drinking again, and the pattern will repeat until you've really given it some careful thought.

You may have rebelled against a parent's alcoholism by avoiding drinking altogether, and the reason for your unyielding opposition to drinking is clear to you. It could still be a handicap to you if you're unable to tolerate anyone who drinks, even moderately.

The Ogre

You may remember hating your father for his meanness, but if you blamed yourself for it, you may not connect your father's behavior with the fact that you yourself are mean. Or, as a rebellion against his meanness, maybe you overdeveloped your sense of generosity, no matter what the cost to you. Still, you don't associate this generosity as a rebellion against your father's mean behavior.

The Sad Sack

You may remember your mother's depression, but if you felt sorry for her, or blamed yourself for it, you may not realize that it's caused you to feel depressed or undeserving of having fun with your friends. If you rebelled against her neediness, you could have become hard and insensitive, as a way of insulating yourself against the suffering of others. Again, the relationship between your parent's depression and your unhappiness is important to recognize if you are to change.

The Obese One

You may remember having an obese family member, but if you felt badly for him or her, or blamed yourself for his or her eating problem, you may not be clear about why you have trouble controlling your weight. You may remember that one of your parents or siblings was self-centered, always demanding admiration. You may not realize that your problem with losing weight and becoming attractive is to avoid threatening your self-centered parent or sibling. You may recall being upset by a parent who continually pressured you to be thin. Did you rebel by overeating? Was defiance your way of signaling to your parent to stop the unrelenting pressure? If your parent withheld food from you to manipulate or punish you, are you still rebelling today by overeating? Think about the connection; it's there if you look.

The Failure

You may remember your father's failures in business, but you may not connect it with your own pattern of continually losing money in the stock market. Your failure with investing may be a way of avoiding showing him up and in this way protecting him from feeling worthless because of his business failings.

Then there are the many people who watched a parent repeatedly fail in business and who very clearly identify this as the reason why they are obsessed with making money. However, they're unaware of why their wealth doesn't make them feel secure. For them, the more they have, the guiltier they feel about being so much better off than the parent who failed. Their guilt unconsciously requires them to expect to lose their wealth as a punishment. As a result they're compelled to make even more money to protect against the fantasy of financial disaster. The last situation puts them in a cycle of making money, then losing it to atone for their guilt, and then using that atonement to feel justified to acquire wealth again.

The Black Sheep

You might remember how your parents worried about the poor performance of your brother or sister, "the black sheep." But because you went through life not ever wanting to disappoint them by outdoing your sibling, you may not see that this was the reason you did poorly at school or, later on, at work. Or you might rebel and be driven to succeed, and you do so to the point that it affects all other aspects of your life, leaving you little time for your family or for pleasure.

The Critical Parent

You may remember being criticized all the time, but not realize that this is causing you to be too critical of others, and be disliked for it. You don't want to be disliked, but you just don't understand what motivates you to *mimic* your parent. But if you *rebelled* you might have developed another unappealing quality, which is the refusal to ever listen to *any* criticism. Or is *accommodation* the way you adapted to being criticized, and so you easily blame yourself for things that aren't your fault, and have still not developed the ability to stick up for yourself?

What Keeps the Truth Hidden

Children bury their heads under the covers when they're afraid of ghosts, and in the same way they bury their unconscious outrage, disgust, and disappointment from their hurtful family experiences. Adults look just a little before turning away when they're approaching a gruesome accident, attempting to limit how horrified they become. Since the truth of our past is often horrifying and painful to us, we are compelled to turn away from it.

We've looked at the pain of accommodation, rebellion, and mimicking. Let's turn now to *idealizing* and see its causes as well as its effects in our lives.

Cutting Some Slack: Idealizing Our Parents and Siblings

Why do we find ourselves viewing our parents or siblings more favorably than our actual experiences with them warrant? There are three main reasons. The first is to keep you from remembering and reexperiencing the pain and sadness associated with the memories of your parents' flaws, and the compromises they caused you to suffer in your life.

The second reason for idealizing our parents and siblings (that is, cutting them some slack) is, as we mentioned, we don't want to reexperience the guilt that they made us feel for hurting them. If we view them in a more favorable light and give them better grades than they deserve, we don't have to.

Finally, if our parents or siblings are easily hurt by criticism and vulnerable to feeling exposed, we'll feel guilty for remembering and/or pointing out their faults or vulnerabilities. In many families, parents want the outside world to think of them as upstanding, moral, well-balanced, and good parents. Obviously such parents would want their mistakes and mistreatments to remain hidden from public view.

That doesn't mean that you'll feel guilty *only* when you openly complain to your parents about their faults. If they're vulnerable to criticism, even *thinking* about their faults can make you feel uneasy, just as if you were having thoughts like killing, stealing, cheating on your spouse, or the like. This is because those thoughts are judged to be wrong or bad. To protect their feelings you'd deny the truth and therefore see them in a better light than deserved. Removing the rose-colored glasses that we wear when idealizing our parents is necessary for us to get to the truth about our family.

What Rose-Colored Glasses Do You Wear?

Think about yourself: *Who*, or even *what*, are you idealizing in your life? Going right to the heart of your family and removing your rose-colored glasses may be hard for you to do right now. If it is, don't do it. If it isn't, go for it. If you decide it's not the time for you to dig deeper there, then look around in other parts of your life. For example, is it a person at work whose faults you don't want to see because you need this person in order to bring a presentation out to your company's newest client? Is it the friend who seems less like a friend and more like a rival whenever there's a new man in your life?

What if You Were the Apple of Their Eye?

What if you were loved and adored by your parents instead of having been mistreated in your childhood? Despite this, you notice that you're having trouble in your adult life. You may think this positive family experience would be an advantage and unlikely to lead to problems in your adult life. But it can. If you thought that being so special caused your sibling or the other parent to feel rejected or inferior, you might go through life with one hand behind your back, limiting your potential in order to make them look better. This in turn relieves your guilt about being preferred. In this way, *positive reinforcement* can lead to a *negative outcome*. Maybe you know someone who was favored by her parents over a brother or a sister. When you think about this person, does it seem that she might be limiting herself at work so that her sibling could get recognition? Did this person ever tell you stories about her academic achievements in school in which she clearly limited herself so the less-favored sibling would shine for his or her academic performance and be seen as the better student?

Another set of problems can also emerge from being loved and adored if your parents' admiration means that they're living through your accomplishments. Living up to extremely high standards in school, sports, career, and the like can become an unwelcome obligation in order to make your parents feel worthwhile. You either have to become a perfectionist in everything you do, or rebel in the opposite way by dropping out or failing in many areas of life. Remember Meg back in Chapter 5? She rebelled against her mother's demands for discipline, and ran her life opposite to her mother's standards, all at a great cost to herself.

Exercise: Now It's Your Turn

Where do you fit into the mix we've just described? Were you the adored child? If you were, can you find any clues to help you solve the problems that caused you to buy this book? Here are some ideas to get your search underway. Do you feel guilty about being preferred over, or outperforming, others? Whom do you defer your success to? Who are you trying to promote, in lieu of yourself? Are you a workaholic who can never relax or take time off? Do you disappoint everyone's expectations of you over and over again, in spite of talent, intellect, and personality? Think about it, but if you get stuck, or it's just too painful, just continue reading with the knowledge that it may not be the right time or place for you to be doing the detective work and that reading about this is as far as you need to go right now.

Moving Ahead

In Chapter 8 we look at your life as a trial in which your freedom from the psychological jail in which you find yourself is at stake. You may see yourself as a prisoner in your life today, but you are also the keeper of all the keys that unlock the door to your freedom in the future.

CHAPTER 8

Crime, Punishment, and Psychological Jail

IMAGINE THAT YOU HAVE BEEN arrested, convicted, and punished for someone else's crime. Someone in your family committed the crime and you ended up getting punished. If you're trapped in behavior you hate, that's really what has happened to you. You're trapped in a place I call "psychological jail."

Your Arrest

In the novel by Franz Kafka, *The Trial*, a law-abiding bank clerk is suddenly arrested and spends the rest of his life defending himself against unspecified charges. That's similar to the psychological experience of a very guilty person. Like any imprisonment, it begins with an accusation. But in this case, you make it against yourself or you allow someone else to make it and you never speak in your own defense. Say your parents have tried to manipulate you to *accommodate* their defects by accusing you of wounding them, ruining their lives, making them suffer, causing them to sacrifice for you, or being selfish. They reinforce their sense of suffering by pouting, withdrawing, shouting out of control, rejecting, pleading, and looking to heaven to ask, "What have I done to deserve this?" And every time you try to save yourself from giving in to their manipulations, they repeat these maneuvers. You have natural urges and inclinations to defend yourself from the false charges of which you are accused, but these urges are thwarted by these continual barrages. It's as though you're being forced to bear false witness . . . against yourself.

Your Confession

Over and over again the accusations are repeated. Different words and different actions may be used, but all of them are designed to get you to confess and submit to the mercy of your parents. And because their accusations that you are wounding them continue for many years, it's hard for you to assume that their behavior is just a temporary aberration, as your response might be to a bad day at work or for having lost money in the stock market. Because of your exposure to their repeated guilt trips, you finally make (internal) confessions of guilt.

Your Conviction

Your internal confessions eventually create a mountain of emotional evidence against you. As a result you become convinced that you have done something wrong—guilty as charged! And what exactly is criminal (or wrong)? Pursuing one or more of your normal behaviors or goals? Being attractive? Assertive? Successful with people? Successful in a career or with parenting? In your mind, pursuing one (or all of them) is wrong because doing so threatens your flawed parent or sibling. There! You feel that you *do* deserve to be punished, or sentenced.

Your Sentencing

And so you *are* sentenced. For the rest of your life you'll atone for your crime by restricting your freedom to pursue your own goals. To add to your punishment, you may not discuss the case. Do so and your guilt will increase (because you're in danger of humiliating your parents by exposing the truth about how they inappropriately acted victimized by you).

A different kind of punishment awaits those who become defiant and rebel (instead of appeasing or accommodating). The defiant ones are punished by becoming the outcasts. They're outlaws, shunned by others for antisocial behavior (defiance, stubbornness, self-centeredness, uncooperativeness, and/or being provocative). Any attempt to escape this prison, via the pursuit of normal goals and ambitions, will result in a painful renewal of guilt and restrictions. This is psychological jail. The key that locks the door is self-blame; the key that unlocks it is self-knowledge.

Your False Imprisonment

When people with a conscience feel they've done something wrong, they feel they should be punished. If they are punished, they feel relief. What's the psychological equivalent of being punished? Not to have the freedom to enjoy your life. You'll suffer, resent your lack of freedom, but you'll be unable to change it.

But what if your jail time were the result of being falsely accused of a crime? You'd fight to get out because you'd know you had done nothing wrong. The psychological equivalent of this is to free yourself from a *false* sense of guilt, and all the self-imposed restrictions that go along with that. In other words, you'd feel perfectly fine pursuing your life goals. Release from your psychological jail is the goal of this book.

Exercise: Now It's Your Turn

You stand accused. Of what? Only you know. Here's your chance not just to be the accused but to also be your own greatest defense attorney. Write down what you know, or what you believe you are being accused of in your family. When you're done, you then get to be your own jury: guilty or not guilty? And if you're not guilty, who is? A list will make it clearer to you who is.

Moving Ahead

Once again, I stop to remind you that if you're not up to this exercise, simply move on to Chapter 9. In Chapter 9, if you've ever asked yourself "Why do I feel like a victim?" you'll start to have your answer.

Why Do You Feel Like a Victim?

DO YOU KNOW ANYONE FOR whom the glass is always half empty? If you do, you know a victim. Are they envious of others, always being mistreated, blaming others for their unhappiness? You know a victim. Why do people put themselves in such an unpleasant role? Let's go back to jail again.

Someone who commits a crime such as stealing is dealt with by our legal system. But what about crimes that are committed internally, such as hurting others by being attractive, independent, accomplished, well liked, successful in a career and marriage, and the like? Your own internal legal system will send you to psychological jail, and in this case the sentence is for you to suffer as a victim. Recall the many real-life stories that have already been presented.

Let's look at some illustrative examples.

Pathological Jealousy: Committing the Crime, Becoming the Victim

The prosecution in the O. J. Simpson trial introduced pathological jealousy as the motive for the murder of Simpson's former wife and a companion of hers. What is the meaning of the term *pathological jealousy*? How does it relate to being a victim? What if you were having an affair? Chances are you'd feel disloyal to your spouse, and most likely also guilty.

To assuage your guilt, you'd punish yourself by feeling *irrationally* mistreated, even betrayed by your spouse. This way, instead of feeling like the one who has wronged someone else, *you are the one who feels wronged*. This is true even though your spouse has really done nothing to you. Instead of feeling guilty, you feel betrayed and victimized. The greater your sense of guilt, the more rage you'll feel toward your spouse. This rage signals how mistreated you feel by your spouse. Therefore, in this context, rage is a sign of how *guilty* you feel, not how *angry*. Does it seem paradoxical that rather than feeling remorseful or apologetic toward the person you hurt, you feel *angry*? What might account for this? The example of my client Mark will help you understand more about the motives for this behavior.

■ MARK ■

Mark was playing a rejection game. Mark had an affair. Because of it he felt so guilty toward his girlfriend that he pushed *her* into having an affair with a friend of his. This was an act of atonement or self-punishment on Mark's part that backfired. Why? When Mark's girlfriend started to date his friend, she began resisting going out with Mark. This caused Mark to go into a violent rage and beat her up. What was the reason for this? After all, hadn't he rejected *her* by having an affair? Hadn't he put her up to dating his friend? Clearly, being rejected *by* her shouldn't have motivated his anger toward her. It didn't. He was actually responding to powerful feelings of guilt caused by having hurt her, and he felt the need to be punished for it by suffering similar feelings of rejection from her.

What drew Mark to this violence? Mark's childhood was spent in the company of his needy and overinvolved mother. Whenever she felt disappointed by him, she acted hurt. Therefore Mark became oversolicitous of her feelings. If he ignored what she needed and instead focused on his own needs, he experienced guilt toward her. As an adult, Mark would call his mother, but his mother complained that Mark "didn't call frequently enough." When he would visit her, she'd whine that "it wasn't sooner."

To solve his guilt about neglecting his mother, Mark would act victimized by her. How does this look? If Mark came home from being out with his friends, he would get angry with his mother for not doing something he had requested of her. Even if it was something insignificant like not cooking what he liked to eat. How did this help Mark? To relieve *his* guilt about neglecting her (by being with his friends instead of her), Mark made *himself* feel neglected by his mother.

And when you think about it, this is exactly what happened with Mark's girlfriend. Unconsciously, Mark felt that by having an affair he was rejecting (neglecting) her. By feeling enraged when she stopped dating him, he made *himself* feel rejected by her to relieve his guilt for hurting her. Mark became enraged when she stopped dating him and made *himself* feel rejected.

From Mark's example, you can see that violence toward a partner can often occur without any apparent provocation. Instead, it's the result of severe unconscious guilt feelings that came from hurting the other person and having to deny it. The stronger your sense of guilt toward your partner, the more violent your anger toward that person. The rage and violence reflect how hurt you are by your partner and serve to exonerate you from having hurt her or him. ▪

Other Causes of Violence
toward a Loved One

Violence toward a loved one may be motivated by causes other than jealousy. For example, if you are extremely sensitive to rejection, having been severely rejected in your childhood, you might overreact and become violent if you are rejected in your current life. Or, if you have been physically brutalized by a parent, you might do the same to a loved one in order to help yourself forget the pain of having been the victim of brutality. Watching someone *else* suffer keeps *you* as far away as possible from the memories of your childhood suffering. And finally, if one of your parents brutalized the other, you might learn by example to repeat the same behavior toward your partner. The *mimicking* of your parent's negative behavior keeps you from feeling sorry for him or her, because in this way you are no better than your parent.

In the section on pathological jealousy, Mark got himself sentenced to psychological jail to suffer victimization at the hands of the person he hurt. Let's look at a case where the sentence is to suffer envy.

▮ SARAH ▮

Sarah was a victim of envy. Sarah was an attractive, educated professional who was married to a great guy. Unfortunately, she was unable to feel happy with him. She got into frequent fights with him, especially when she began feeling they were getting too close. She was also unable to sustain her friendships with women because she always ended up feeling unreasonably jealous of them. For these reasons, Sarah hated herself.

As therapy progressed, I learned that during her childhood, Sarah's sister had been terribly jealous of her for being their father's favorite. The result was that when Sarah got older, she tried to play down the close relationship between her and her dad. How did she do this? Mainly by creating distance from him. Now let's go back to Sarah's problems with her husband. At first she tried convincing me that their fights were his fault. But as therapy continued, it became clear that Sarah was repeating the pattern she had with her father in her relationship with her husband. Whenever Sarah tried to become close with a woman friend, the fights between her and her husband became more numerous. Why? Sarah's motive for fighting with her husband was to keep other women from feeling envious of her. This was the same tactic she used to keep her sister from feeling envious of Sarah's relationship their father.

As an adult, Sarah's women friends became her substitute sister. Whenever one of them was unsuccessful with a man, or was having problems with a husband, Sarah's guilt (due to her successful, happy married life) would intensify. To relieve her guilt, Sarah suffered greatly by making herself feel *envious* of her women friends. This helped in two ways: It offset Sarah's fear that they would feel jealous of her, and it reduced her guilt.

When Sarah realized that it wasn't her intention to make her sister jealous, that she was not to blame for the fact that her father favored her, and that her sister's jealousy was also not her fault, Sarah stopped provoking fights with her husband. She also began feeling happier with him. With her women friends, things also changed. Sarah no longer felt obligated to make herself feel envious of them in order to atone for feeling better off than they were. When she reached that point, Sarah's relationships with these women became much more steady, fulfilling, and fun.

■ MARTIN ■

Martin was burdened by his jealous brother. Martin was a very successful professional man who complained to me that he couldn't pursue his interests, relax, or feel happy if he thought that others around him were unhappy. Instead, he felt compelled to solve everyone else's problems.

During one session, Martin told me about a very interesting dream he'd had the night before. In it, he was soaring, happily, over a city, but then inexplicably he had to descend into dark canyons. In the next dream scene he and his brother Tim won the lottery, leaving both of them with an equal amount of money, but Martin allowed his brother to swindle him out of some of his money, resulting in Tim's having more.

Martin's first thoughts about the dream were about how happy he was to be free to fly, that all of his goals could be easily achieved. However, when he had to descend into the dark canyons, he became unhappy and pessimistic. I asked him if he thought there might be a connection between this part of the dream and the section about his brother. He began to recall childhood problems with Tim, who was four years older and always picking on him. Compared to Tim, a streetwise, unsophisticated, and below-average student, Martin was an exceptional student and athlete. Martin said that his father, a blue-collar worker, preferred Tim because Tim was more like him. As an example of this, Martin emphasized that his father went to all of Tim's basketball games and was more responsive to Tim than to him. Martin felt like a victim.

We continued discussing the dream. Martin explained that his mother, who was an intellectual and had been the valedictorian of her high school, strongly valued education. I asked him what he thought was his mother's

attitude toward him and his brother. Martin said that his
mother disdained Tim's macho quality and admired
Martin for his interest in reading and his outstanding
academic performance.

I was curious about Martin's assumption that his
father, who was obsessed by sports, favored Tim in spite of
Martin's superior athletic ability. After all, Martin had
been the star basketball player on the best team in the
state. This stopped Martin in his tracks. He said that he
had never before entertained the possibility that his father
admired him. "Why not?" I asked. Martin told me it was
possible that he was worried that, if that were true, Tim
would resent him even more than he already did for being
his mother's favorite.

A more recent example of Tim's jealousy of Martin
occurred three years earlier, when Tim and his wife visited
Martin in California. During the visit Tim never once said
anything complimentary about Martin's fabulous house
and lifestyle, causing Martin to become terribly upset. I
asked him why that omission was so upsetting and Martin
thought about it. Then he said that it showed how resentful
and jealous Tim was of Martin's success and wealth.

I returned to the dream and asked how it might relate
to the family experiences he just told me about. Martin
said that descending into the dark canyons represented his
need to spoil his success in life because it made his brother
so intensely jealous. I pointed out that to relieve his guilt
over his brother's jealousy he not only made sure that he
and his brother had equal wealth from the lottery, but he
also allowed Tim to swindle him and end up with more.
When he insisted that their father favored Tim, he made
himself feel like a victim to offset the advantage of being
admired by his father *and* preferred by his mother. When
in the dream Martin victimized himself by having his

brother swindle him so that he would have less money than his brother, he relieved his guilt about Tim's jealousy of his success with wealth.

Throughout our lives we encounter people who are jealous of us. If you sat down and thought about it you could probably make a fairly extensive list of people from your past who you sensed wanted what you had and made it clear either in obvious ways or perhaps in not such obvious ways. And then there are the people who just bring out our worst and most jealous selves. By understanding why we become jealous, what's underneath it for us, we can deal with it and have healthier relationships with friends and family in our future.

LLOYD

Lloyd was unable to make demands. Lloyd was a tough businessman who couldn't ask anyone to do anything for him in a calm way. Whenever he had to make a request of almost anyone, he became very angry. Even with his employees, who knew he was in authority and would do whatever he asked, Lloyd acted this way.

What was this about? Lloyd said that asking someone else to do something made *him* feel put upon. "Wouldn't it make more sense for the *employee* to feel imposed on instead?" I asked. He laughed, readily agreed, and thus began his exploration into his odd response.

Strangely enough, Lloyd felt he was truly burdening or imposing on others when requesting something from them. On the surface he appeared angry, but in fact he was really feeling guilty about making demands of others. Therefore, he punished himself by making himself feel the victim as payment for thinking he was victimizing others.

Chances are we all know a Lloyd. Maybe we've worked for one, maybe we're married to one. And then there's always the chance that we actually are one ourselves.

If you have a hard time when you have to ask someone to do something for you, getting a nervous feeling on the inside each time you make a request, or feeling calm inside but giving yourself away by a tightness in your voice, you may be suffering the same kind of self-victimizing as Lloyd was.

Survivor Guilt

"Survivor guilt" is a common experience that causes people to suffer depression and anxiety after they have survived terrible disasters in which others suffered or died. From the stories of soldiers who survived combat when their comrades died, to Holocaust survivors who lived while their families perished, survivor guilt is irrational when the survivor had nothing to do with the misfortune of those who died. Still, in spite of being happy to be alive, survivors feel unworthy because they survived. How is survivor guilt connected to what we've been talking about? Children experience a similar guilt when they have hurt their parents or siblings (Martin and Sarah). Many people have experiences from childhood that make them predisposed to blame themselves when things go wrong. (The blame is unreasonable, too.) These people are likely to experience great emotional problems when surviving tragedies in which others perished.

▧   CASEY   ▧

Casey was punishing himself in his marriage. Casey came to see me because of long-standing problems in his marriage, but also because of depression. During the next few months I learned that both problems were connected with an incident that occurred during the Vietnam War. He had been leading his troops on a reconnaissance mission and had suggested to Jim, one of his officers, that he investigate an enemy area where the Americans had suffered heavy casualties.

Jim preferred to take one particular route, but Casey disagreed and told him to take a different one, which resulted in the deaths of that officer and several other soldiers. As an experienced commander who had seen lots of combat, he always felt badly about the loss of any of his men, but he was unaware that this incident had caused him to feel excessively guilty. As those memories came back he began to sob and told me that he had been very close to Jim. As he went on he told me that he felt terrible about depriving Jim's wife and children of their husband and father, and he chastised himself for not going along with the alternative plan Jim originally suggested to him.

I said to him that for years he had punished himself by fighting with his wife, feeling victimized by her, and remaining depressed for all these years. The purpose was to deprive himself of the satisfactions in life that he thought he had been responsible for depriving Jim of. Over the next two weeks his depression improved, and he began to explore with me the ways he had been provoking his wife.

Casey's survivor's guilt had its roots in actual combat, but sometimes it can be tied to something quite different but just as difficult for us to cope with. This was the case with George. ▪

▪ **GEORGE** ▪

George was guilty about good health. A change in George's life made it possible for him to face his powerful feelings of survivor guilt. Up until his brother died, George had a hard time feeling happy and successful in life. George was capable and talented, but he was also burdened by a strong sense of survivor guilt toward his brother, who suffered from a severe physical handicap. This handicap prevented him from living a full life and George, feeling that it was unfair that he had so much compared to his brother, felt guilty.

These feelings of guilt interfered with George's ability to feel happy. Therapy helped him achieve moderate strides toward his goal of allowing more joy in his life, but after most advances George would experience some setbacks. Complaining a lot, feeling pessimistic about his future, George denied that he had accomplished anything. I pointed out that his negative outlook was helping him to *not* feel so guilty toward his brother and that expressing his negative feelings was almost like talking directly to his brother, telling him to not feel so badly about his life since George too was miserable. Understanding this relieved George's guilt and helped him to feel happier.

George began to feel even better, and more consistently, too, when his brother died. At first he felt embarrassed admitting that he was relieved that his brother was dead. However, after overcoming this embarrassment, George described how much easier it was to no longer have to observe his brother's terrible life and feel pity and sadness for him. Not being able to do anything about his brother's suffering was what was most painful for George. Now that his brother's ordeal was over, so was George's. It was now safer for him to be happy and successful.

Death doesn't always bring the relief of survivor guilt that it brought to George. When there is the ongoing sadness over the thought that your sibling died without ever realizing his or her full potential, often survivor guilt lingers for a long time.

Sometimes when our own circumstances mirror a parent's, our survivor guilt takes hold of our lives in a different way. Steve's cardiac case study is an example.

STEVE

Steve was not going to enjoy his life. Steve came to me for therapy following a severe heart attack because he had become depressed. After undergoing successful bypass surgery, Steve was told that he'd have to retire. He would, however, still be able to be moderately active: play golf, go for walks, travel, and have sex with his wife. Despite the fact that Steve was relieved that he didn't have to return to his very stressful career, and that disability insurance took care of his financial needs, Steve still became depressed. Why?

Years earlier, Steve's father had suffered a heart attack and he hadn't adjusted well to his changed circumstances. In fact, as a result of excessive anxiety about his survival, Steve's father became what Steve called a "cardiac cripple." Completely unable to enjoy his remaining years, he nevertheless refused the recommended bypass surgery, choosing instead to live every
day in fear of dying.

On a few occasions, however, he complained to Steve of chest pain. One such time, Steve told him to call his doctor and have it checked out immediately. But his father, in denial, assumed it was indigestion and did nothing. He died a short time later. Even though Steve had told his father to contact his doctor immediately, he still experienced an irrational sense of blame for his father's death. Steve felt that he should have told his father that his chest pain was most likely caused by his heart disease. Had he told him, Steve believed, his father would have been more inclined to see his doctor.

Although irrational, powerful guilt feelings still plagued Steve. Not only did these feelings make him obsess about what he could have done differently, they also interfered with Steve's ability to take advantage of the opportunity to enjoy the rest of *his* life. His father's inability to manage his life successfully following his heart attack, combined with Steve's (irrational) sense of responsibility, made it hard for Steve to feel that he deserved to enjoy his own life. Steve was suffering from survivor's guilt as a result of his having escaped his father's fate. When Steve was no longer able to perform in his career, he unconsciously worried that he was letting his family down. This made him feel that he didn't deserve to enjoy retirement.

Exercise: Now It's Your Turn

Psychological jail is a place none of us would choose to be and yet is precisely where many of us find ourselves. Looking at it with our eyes fully open can help us break out. Answering the questions below will start the process. Let's use envy as an example. These questions are specifically about psychological jail and the part that envy plays in putting you there and keeping you there. The first question to ask yourself is, who in the past, and (more important) more recently, has acted hurt, threatened, or envious of you? If, as with Martin and Sarah, one of your family members was very jealous of you, do you in turn make yourself feel envious of others?

- Who do you find yourself envying?
- Why do you envy him or her?

- Who envied *you* in your childhood?
- Who envies you today?
- Which situations in your life provoke you to feel intensely envious of others?

Moving Ahead

We've come a long way and covered a lot of territory and all in a fairly short time. Next up is the chance to take a clear and honest look at your family members in a way that will let you put their failings into a new perspective. Doing this will continue moving you forward in your quest to be in charge of your own thinking, and acting, and ultimately your life.

CHAPTER 10

Assessing Yourself and Your Family Members

Up until now you've had a chance to review charts offering a quick way to look at the problems in your family that have had a negative effect on your life. You've also read true stories of people whose hidden beliefs led to self-destructive behaviors. As a result, you may have learned not only about the source of your personal problems but also why they've been difficult to overcome.

If you're still not totally clear about your family's failings, the following personality profiles will help you uncover them. Having done so, you'll be empowered to act on your own behalf instead of being controlled by unknown forces. What are personality profiles? Personality profiles are sets of questions that help you to identify the flaws of your family and to learn the real underlying causes of your problems.

Below are a series of questions. Write your answers down so you can refer back to them if you need to. Then, go to the chart titled "What Happened to You When Your Parents and Siblings Acted Badly" and look for the qualities in the chart that match the flaws of your family. You can answer these questions by yourself or with your spouse or friends. Completing these personality profiles with others can help you develop a better understanding of one another's problems and their origins. Seeing how your family experiences shaped you and your partner or friends can promote mutual support and a more caring relationship.

WHAT HAPPENED TO YOU WHEN YOUR PARENTS AND SIBLINGS ACTED BADLY

Your Parents' or Siblings' Flaw	When You Accommodate	When You Rebel and Protest	When You Mimic and Do to Others What Was Done to You
Excessively controlling and authoritarian	You overrespect authority, are submissive, and excessively obedient.	You are stubborn, defiant, and contrary.	You are bossy, demanding, and expect obedience to you and the rules.
Weak and ineffectual	You have to be strong, take charge, and be in control.	You ignore others' problems and let them flounder.	You are meek and give in to what others want.
Possessive	You are overly loyal, and afraid to be separate.	You reject demands and keep your distance from those who want you to be close to them.	You suffocate others, and feel easily jealous of attention paid to others, even violently.
Rejecting	You are self-reliant, don't show your feelings, and avoid close relationships.	You demand attention and act destructively, if necessary.	You are indifferent to others and enjoy seeing them hurt.
Overprotective	You are very cautious about doing sports and physical activities.	You are careless, reckless, and a daredevil type.	You see danger everywhere, and restrict your kids.
Underprotective	You take chances and don't notice the usual signs of danger.	You are too cautious and overly alert to danger.	You ignore signs of danger, especially with your children.

Competitive and self-centered	You are afraid to speak up or stand out. You limit your successes with looks, or career, or parenting.	You avoid giving credit and go out of your way to get attention.	You put down others, enjoy their faults, and need to be the center of attention.
Self-effacing and modest	You are uncomfortable highlighting your virtues.	You become boastful, and enjoy taking center stage.	You are self-effacing.
Critical	You have low self-esteem, accept blame easily, and may feel "why try?"	You deny anything is ever your fault.	You are quick to blame others even when they have done no wrong.
Live through your accomplishments	You have to be perfect, and stand out. You are anxious about failing.	You hide your accomplishments, and may deliberately fail.	You expect perfection and are too critical of mistakes.
Overly righteous and disdainful	You highlight your moral failings and may run afoul of the law.	You parade your moral virtues.	You are disdainful of others and highlight their moral flaws.
Amoral	You have trouble following the rules.	You insist on honesty in all your dealings and don't tolerate cheats.	You use people and use any means to get what you want.
Depressed	You feel guilty about being happy. You have to help others in order to feel good.	You are insensitive to and avoid unhappy people.	You complain all the time. No one can make you happy. You always look grim.
Abuse drugs and alcohol	You become very vigilant and try to avoid setting them off. You feel unprotected and have to be the parent.	You hate anyone not in control.	You are unpredictable and explosive. You are attracted to drugs and alcohol.
Abusive	You feel irrationally at fault. You do anything to please.	You fight back as much as possible. You go through life angry, have a chip on your shoulder.	You become a bully and physically abuse others the way you were treated.

Personality Profiles

To discover the most damaging and problematic qualities of your parents and siblings, answer the following set of questions. Let's begin with your father. The same exercise can then be reworded to create profiles for your mother, siblings, and other family members important to you during your childhood.

ASSESSING YOUR FATHER

1. Were there behaviors that you hated in your father? If so, what were they?
2. What situations in your family made these behaviors worse?
3. What situations in your family made your father behave better?
4. What did you think was your role in those situations in which your father behaved badly?
5. If you wished that someone else could be your father, what qualities did that person have that were different from those of your father?
6. Who were the people outside your immediate family who made a positive difference in your life? What qualities did they have that were lacking in your parent, and what did these people offer you?

ASSESSING YOUR MOTHER, SIBLINGS, AND OTHER FAMILY MEMBERS

Once you've answered these questions about your father, complete a personality profile for your mother. Then do one for each sibling. Finally, include any other family members (grandparents, aunts and uncles, cousins) who were significant during your childhood. Now complete the following personality profile for yourself.

ASSESSING YOURSELF

Ask yourself the following questions:

1. Are there any behaviors in yourself that you hate? If so, what are they?
2. If you could be anyone else, who would you choose, and why?
3. What provokes the behavior you hate in yourself?
4. What makes your behavior worse, and what makes it better?
5. Do you find yourself repeating behaviors you hate that you remember seeing in your parents or siblings?
6. Write a letter to your parents and/or siblings explaining what you wish had been different in your relationship with them during your childhood. You *do not* have to send or show them the letter. Many people think they must confront the family member or members who caused them grief, and while it might be helpful to do so, it's not always necessary. If you *do* choose to confront family members, you need to do it constructively so that their negative behavior doesn't become more rigid. Chances are that they will deny their responsibility and accuse you of being at fault (just as they did when you were a child).

Having answered these questions, you're now ready to find your parents and/or siblings on the chart called "What Happened to You When Your Parents and Siblings Acted Badly," and see where you fit. Then find *yourself* on the chart "Checking Out Your Symptoms." This should help you to understand how you developed the behavior you hate and to see if it's a result of accommodating, rebelling, or mimicking your parent and/or sibling. Remember, you weren't the *cause* of your parents' and/or siblings' unhappiness. You were the *victim* of their problems. That means that you're not responsible for their flaws. Appreciating this truth will allow you to feel less guilty toward your family and more deserving of doing well for yourself, and ultimately, it will allow you to rid yourself of the behavior you hate.

SAMPLE ASSESSMENTS: ONE MAN'S STORY

The following sample assessments by one man of his father, mother, and brother illustrate how this process works.

Assessment of the Father

1. Were there behaviors that you hated in your father? If so, what were they?

"The behavior I hated most in my father was his inability to feel confident and successful at anything he tried. He continually failed in his business and acted depressed about his inability to make money. He was always in debt. His morale and self-image were so bad that he became overly preoccupied with his plight and couldn't focus on the other people in his family. As a result, he tended to withdraw by watching TV.

"He almost never complimented me, or others. He smoked and overate, and he was unable to overcome either habit even when his health was bad. The way he dealt with his poor self-image was to try to make himself the center of attention or to insist that he was right. He was quick to see fault in others, but was defensive or in denial about his own."

2. What situations made his behavior worse?

"He had a difficult time making a living, and this sense of frustration worsened whenever he had business or financial pressures. He borrowed money from relatives and resented both them and himself for it. This added to his low self-esteem, which caused him to overeat, lose his temper, and become even more withdrawn. He would often complain, 'Things are too much for me.' When he was in such a state of mind, he might break down and cry during an argument."

CHECKING OUT YOUR SYMPTOMS

The Behavior That You Hate in Yourself	When the Behavior Results from Pleasing Your Parents or Siblings	When It Results from Rebelling and Protesting Against What They Expect	When It Results from Mimicking the Flaw of Your Parents or Siblings
You are fat and can't lose weight.	1. Your parent or sibling is self-centered about his/her looks and jealous of people who are attractive. 2. They need you to eat in order to feel fulfilled.	1. He or she is obsessed about your eating habits and needs for you to be thin. 2. He or she withholds food or desserts as punishment.	Your parent is fat and suffers because of it. You feel sorry for him or her, and may feel that you contributed to it
You are shy, insecure, and inadequate.	Your parents or siblings need to brag and show off in order to feel worthwhile.	They live through you, needing you to be strong and the center of attention. You rebel by acting shy and insecure	He or she is insecure and you feel sorry for him or her.
You show off and have to be the center of attention.	They live through your accomplishments.	They prefer that you be seen and not heard, stay in the background. You rebel by showing off.	He or she is a big show off and needs to be the center of attention.
You whine and complain all the time.	1. He or she needs to feel superior. You give him or her a reason to be contemptuous of you.	He or she resents you and is unresponsive to your needs	He or she or a sibling acts like a victim, suffers, and complains all the time.

CHECKING OUT YOUR SYMPTOMS (continued)

The Behavior That You Hate in Yourself	When the Behavior Results from Pleasing Your Parents or Siblings	When It Results from Rebelling and Protesting Against What They Expect	When It Results from Mimicking the Flaw of Your Parents or Siblings
You are too obedient and compliant, and give in quickly to others. You don't think for yourself.	He or she is too authoritarian, controlling, bossy, and rigid.	Your parent expects you to be a rebel and nonconformist. You rebel with compliant behavior.	He or she is a "yes man" and does what he or she is told.
You are too controlling and authoritarian.	They are ineffectual and out of control. You take over and run the show.	Your parent expects you to be compliant, to compromise and give in.	Your parent was rigid and controlling.
You are stubborn and defiant and refuse to give in or compromise.	Your parent expects you to be independent and not be influenced by others.	Your parent is too controlling and authoritarian.	Your parent is stubborn.
You are aloof and avoid closeness with others.	1. Your parent is rejecting and cold. 2. One parent competes with you for the attention of the other parent.	Your parent is too possessive and wants you to be closer to him or her than to anyone else.	Your parent is aloof, and avoids closeness with others.
You are needy and dependent.	Your parent babies you and is uncomfortable with your independence.	He or she is rejecting and cold, and wants you to be emotionally distant from him or her.	He or she is a dependent and needy person.

You			
You refuse to listen to others.	Your parent admires people who are totally independent of and uninfluenced by others.	1. Your parent is excessively critical of you. 2. Your parent is excessively dependent on you (for advice).	Your parent never listens to others and can't take advice.
You yell all the time.	Your parent acts contemptuous and superior to others. Your yelling helps them to feel superior.	1. Your parent doesn't pay attention to you. 2. Your parent can't stand it when you express your feelings.	Your parent screams all the time.
You steal or cheat.	Your parent needs to feel morally superior.	Your parent deprived you or used you. You rebel by stealing or cheating to get what you want.	Your parent is dishonest, cheats others, and steals.
You are very mistrustful of others.	Your parent expects you to trust and depend mainly on him or her.	Your parent is overly naïve, trusting, and easily taken advantage of.	Your parent is mistrustful and paranoid.
You select friends who tend to reject you.	Your parent is jealous of the attention you pay to others. He or she expects devotion from you.	Your parent lives through you and needs you to have perfect relationships.	One parent rejects the other parent. Your sibling is rejected by others.
You avoid showing your feelings.	Your parent is insensitive to your feelings, lacks empathy, and/or is rejecting.	Your parent or sibling is depressed and needy of sympathy and care. You rebel by not showing your feelings.	One parent is indifferent to the other's pain or complaints.
You rescue people and feel overly sorry for people and animals.	Your parent is needy, unhappy, or mistreated, and needs attention.	Your parent is indifferent to the suffering of others.	Your parent is a "do gooder" and rescuer.

CHECKING OUT YOUR SYMPTOMS (continued)

The Behavior That You Hate in Yourself	When the Behavior Results from Pleasing Your Parents or Siblings	When It Results from Rebelling and Protesting Against What They Expect	When It Results from Mimicking the Flaw of Your Parents or Siblings
You are never satisfied with your achievements. You need to be perfect.	Your parent lives through your accomplishments, and expects perfection.	Your parent makes fun of your mistakes, and can't stand anyone to be successful.	Your parent has to be perfect and drives him or herself at every task.
You are extremely vigilant for signs of emotional instability or intoxication.	Your parent is emotionally unpredictable, and may have been a drug or alcohol user.	Your parent is in denial whenever a crisis occurs and doesn't respond appropriately.	Your parent is continually anxious, vigilant, worried, or paranoid.
You are a chronic liar.	1. Your parent is vulnerable to exposure of his/her flaws. 2. He or she needs to always look good to the world.	1. Your parent is too moralistic or rigid about telling the truth, no matter what the cost. 2. Your parent is quick to point out your flaws or make fun of you.	Your parent is a liar and never tells the truth.

3. What situations made his behavior better?
"Paying attention to him made him feel more important. He felt especially good when he could be the center of attention, when people laughed at his jokes, or when they complimented him."

4. What was your role in those situations in which he acted badly?
"Whenever I was successful at something and got attention from the rest of my family, he became more dejected and withdrew from me. He never played sports with me or showed interest in my school activities. For example, he didn't come to any of my high school performances, and didn't come to my college graduation. He said that he couldn't get away because of his business, but I knew better and it hurt me."

5. If you wished someone else could be your father, what qualities did that person have that were different from your father's?
"I wished that my uncle could be my father because he exuded self-confidence, was effective with people, and was successful in his career. As a result, everyone in the family admired him. Life seemed easy for him in contrast with how burdened my father was. My uncle was knowledgeable about people, politics, and philosophy. I thought that if he could have been my father instead I would have been happier."

6. Who were the others in your life who made a difference to you?
"Teachers who appreciated my accomplishments and encouraged me to accomplish my goals. It seemed to make it easier for me to be successful in school, sports, and a career when I had a mentor. I guess I was looking for a father substitute who was both self-confident and supportive."

Summary of the Assessment of the Father   You can see that this man's father, who was a failure in business, was self-centered and competitive to compensate for feelings of inadequacy and insecurity. The result? He felt threatened by his son's accomplishments and was unable to compliment or give attention to him. This caused his son to assume that *his* successes intensified his father's insecurity. As a result he felt guilty about doing well in school and being popular. Finding mentors who served as positive father figures made it easier for him to pursue his goals.

Read on to see how the same man continued with his family profiles. Next up, his mother.

Assessment of the Mother
1. Were there behaviors you hated in your mother? If so, what were they?
"My mother seemed unhappy and disappointed with my father and made excuses for his inadequacies. She complained a lot and seemed to always need cheering up. So I spent a lot of time talking with her."

2. What made her behavior worse?
"She worried more when my father was withdrawn and got caught up in his worries about money. She seemed burdened by the need to make my father feel better. Even when things seemed all right she always had some physical problem to complain about."

3. What made her behavior better?
"She seemed happier with me and with my relatives than with my father. She enjoyed my accomplishments, admired my ambition, and enjoyed talking to me. When I performed well in school and sports, or was complimented by neighbors, teachers, or relatives, she was more upbeat. She also seemed

to enjoy the time she spent with her brother or sister more than with my father."

4. *What was your role in those situations in which she acted badly?*
"When I didn't pay enough attention to her, she became less happy."

5. *If you wished someone else could be your mother, what qualities did that person have that were different from your mother's?*
"I wished that one of my friend's mothers was my mother because she seemed happier, self-assured, and less needy of attention, and she didn't complain. A friend of the family was also like that. She was always glad to see me and didn't need to hear I had accomplished something special in order to like me. She was more upbeat."

Summary of the Assessment of the Mother   This mother seemed needy, complained a lot, and was unhappy with her husband. Focusing on her son for satisfaction, she was disappointed when he didn't give her enough attention. The result? Her son felt obligated to cheer her up and do things she could be proud of. This caused him to grow up avoiding anyone who complained or was needy and unhappy.

Assessment of the Sibling
The same man continues with his sibling's profile now.

1. *Where there behaviors that you hated in your sibling? If so, what were they?*
"My brother was much younger than I was, and my relationship with him was more that of a parent than a brother. What I disliked was having to take care of him because my parents worked. It wasn't that I disliked him but that I

resented having to come home right after school to look after him. There were many times that I hated him because he
interfered with my spending time with my friends."

2. *What made this behavior worse, and what made it better?*
"When my parents were unavailable, I had to take time out
of my life to do things with my brother like helping him with
his homework, and making him dinner. When my parents
were available and took over, that freed me to do more of the
things I enjoyed."

3. *What did you think was your role in those situations where
your sibling behaved badly?*
"He actually didn't behave badly. It was that I resented having to be a parent substitute for him. He always looked up to
me and wanted to tag along. It was the responsibility."

Summary of the Assessment of the Sibling
This man felt resentful about having to take care of his mother
and his brother. The result? He avoided anyone who was
needy and dependent.

This next sample assessment shows how the same man used
the personality profile to discover his *own* mind-set.

ASSESSING YOURSELF
1. *Is there a behavior in yourself that you hate? If so, what
is it?*
"What I hate most in myself is the trouble I have enjoying my
achievements. I don't seem to have trouble being successful,
but I worry whether I have done enough and, as a result, don't
seem to enjoy my sense of accomplishment. I also have trouble feeling close to people that I care about. If they have problems, I feel I have to help them, to make sure they do things

well. I have difficulty not being helpful, even when this interferes with what I want to do for myself."

2. What situations in your life make the behavior you hate worse?
"When I do things well, I tend to feel more worried than happy. I don't like to be involved with needy people because I feel obligated to help them. I am intolerant of incompetent or whiny people because they make me feel I have to take care of them."

3. Which situations in your life make the behavior you hate better?
"When I do things well and am appreciated for it, I feel happy and relaxed. I enjoy being involved with people who are accomplished, independent, and interesting. When I think of my friends, or of the women I've been seriously involved with, I realize they have all been successful and independent. I have the most fun with happy, successful people because I don't have to worry about them."

4. Who are your role models, and what qualities did they have?
"One of my role models was my uncle, who was self-assured, charming, and effective with people. Very little bothered him. He was able to be successful without feeling guilty about it. Also, he never seemed self-conscious when he was admired. He was unusual to me because, unlike so many people I knew, he had a combination of intellectual talent, social skills, and confidence."

5. Do you ever notice treating your children, partner, or others the way you were treated?
"My father was competitive with me—I'm not competitive with my children. My mother manipulated me to be loyal and

involved with her at my own expense—I don't do that with my children. I do find that I am a perfectionist with my children and don't have enough patience with their mistakes. I don't re-member if that was how I was treated. However, I tend to be opinionated with my children like my father was with me."

LETTERS TO THE PARENTS

This same person now writes letters to his parents telling them what he wished had been different in his childhood.

Assessing Yourself: Letter to Father

Dear Dad,

You were so depressed about being a failure that you ignored me. I wish we could have been closer. Maybe that would have happened if you had been more successful in your life. It always bothered me that you constantly wor-ried about money and that you felt you would never be a success. You complained about everything being such a burden for you. This made me feel sorry for you. I felt that you resented my accomplishments because you always had to be the center of attention.

It seemed that you were always changing the subject of conversation to bring it back to yourself. No matter how hard I tired, it was always very difficult to have a conver-sation with you. It bothered me that you would never play ball with me or go for walks with me like my friends' fathers. You never listened to me or gave any importance to my point of view. I grew up feeling like you didn't like me. I could never understand why.

Assessing Yourself: Letter to Mother

Dear Mom,

I wish you had been a happier person. I wish you hadn't complained so much. Your complaining made me feel like I had to reassure you all the time to make you even a little happy. No matter how hard I tried, it was never enough. You were never happy. Also, when I finished graduate school and moved to another city, you made me feel guilty about moving away. It seemed that I had to take care of all your problems, even if it meant never going away, never making a future for myself, or meeting new people. You bragged about me to your friends. I was embarrassed and felt like you were living your life through me. I wish you had let go. And let me feel good about being independent and making my own way, separate from you.

SUMMARY OF *ONE MAN'S STORY* ASSESSMENT

Two or three major issues troubled this man. He felt that his mother derived most of her satisfaction through his achievements. This made him feel he had to perform to make her happy. *Accommodating* to his mother's needs required him to be perfect; if he wasn't he'd feel that he was disappointing her. This also made it hard for him to move away from her. It also accounts for his resenting people who are needy, disorganized, or unhappy, because it makes him feel that he has to rescue them. This was reinforced by his having to take the place of his parents in caring for his younger brother. He has a hard time tolerating mistakes or shortcomings in his wife and children, because this makes him feel that he has to worry about them and be burdened with responsibility for them (the way he felt growing up).

Because his father was a failure and he compensated by acting opinionated, and demanding to be the center of attention, our subject *worried* rather than *enjoyed* his accomplishments. Unconsciously, he believed that worrying instead of feeling happy kept his father from being envious of him.

Our subject enjoys being involved only with successful, competent, and interesting people who can appreciate him without being threatened by his success. These kinds of people would also be self-sufficient and wouldn't need to depend on him the way his mother did.

He is opinionated with his own children, the same way his father was with him. By *mimicking* his father's traits, he prevents himself from feeling that he is a better parent than his father was. Unconsciously, this serves to keep his father from feeling envious of him. Additionally, behaving with his own children the way his father behaved with him would spare him the pain of remembering how his father treated him.

Using Your New Self-Knowledge

Here is where you usually find an exercise called "Now It's Your Turn," but simply going through the chapter and doing all the work asked of you was the exercise.

Moving Ahead

Having completed your own family profiles, use the charts we've been using throughout the book to trace the source of your problems. You'll be able to understand the specific causes of your current difficulties. This awareness should help you to better understand how your actions are the result of past experiences with your parents and/or your siblings.

Once you've finished your family profiles, you'll find it easier to benefit from the next two chapters on why people are stuck in areas of success, relationships, and parenting.

CHAPTER 11

Overcoming Accommodation, Rebellion, and Mimicking

Now that you're clear about your hidden motives, you'll be able to progress toward your goals. But sometimes, despite all the positive changes you've made, you'll catch yourself backsliding. At that moment, take stock of your current situation by asking yourself, Is an important person in my life (a friend, co-worker, relative, boss) provoking me in ways that are similar to how a family member provoked me in my childhood? If the answer is yes, it will now be easy for you to see the connection, realize the irrational effect it's having on you, and move to overcome it.

What issues limit your goals in the areas of success? of relationships? of parenting? To discover them, start by looking again at the chart entitled "Checking Out Your Symptoms" in Chapter 10 on page 117. The chart will help you assess the complaints that you have about yourself and see how they developed as a result of accommodating, rebelling, or mimicking the flaws of your parent or sibling. In the same way you used earlier charts, scan down the left column and locate the specific behavior you dislike in yourself. The columns that follow will explain the origins of your problems in relation to the behavior of your family. As in previous charts, some will be based on accommodation and others on rebellion and mimicking. Finally, I'll explain how your new awareness will enable you to overcome them. For instance, in the leftmost column is the behavior "You are shy, insecure, and inadequate." The next column over you'll see that if *accommodation* was responsible for your shyness, it was to not threaten a parent or sibling who liked to brag and show off. Moving over one more column, you see that if *rebellion* was responsible for your shyness, it was to protest against a parent or sibling who needed to be the center of attention. Finally, in the last column, we learn that if *mimicking* was responsible, you felt sorry for the parent or sibling who was insecure and shy and mimicked that quality in order to not feel that you were better off emotionally.

Applying Your New Knowledge

Now that you've answered the Self-Assessment Questions in Chapter 10 and have reviewed the chart "Checking Out Your Symptoms" above, it's time to actually apply your new knowledge to your real life. Reading this material may help you to better apply the charts and enhance your understanding of your problem.

1. You notice that you put down other people. Examine your motive for doing this. If your father put you down because he was threatened by your sense of confidence, you might be mimicking him in order to be less effective with people than he was. What do you do, if, in spite of your new knowledge and progress, you start to slip back into the habit putting down others? Think about your current personal, work, or family relationships. Try to assess whether anyone is acting threatened by you the way your father did.

2. You act silly or make mistakes in front of others. You probably now recognize that you did this to accommodate an insecure parent, one who compensated for his failings of inferiority by acting superior to you and others. Or you could be rebelling against a parent who needed you to be perfect.

3. You consistently defy people in authority.   This was your way to rebel and protest against a controlling, domineering parent or sibling. Knowing this, you will find it easier to not interpret every suggestion, request, and rule as enslaving. The result? You'll find it easier to cooperate, to work, and to socialize more effectively. Instead of negative and angry reactions from others, you may even be surprised to find that you are appreciated and well liked.

4. You are afraid to speak up, assert your point of view, or negotiate from a position of strength.   Assertive behavior threatened a domineering parent or sibling. Because you assume that it will similarly threaten others, you avoid assertive behavior, even when you know it would benefit you. You now know that you hold yourself back this way because you irrationally worry about hurting the other person. The result? The smallest steps you take to promote yourself will result in others' respecting you more and that will encourage you to continue your new constructive pattern.

5. You are too reserved.   If you're afraid to be engaging with people because your parent was overly critical or rejecting when you were friendly and charming, you now have the tools to change that behavior. You know that your parent's flaw wasn't your fault and, armed with that knowledge, you'll no longer feel guilty about promoting your personal skills with people.

6. You demand perfection of yourself and others.   If you're never satisfied with any of your accomplishments, you're not able to see that your motivation was to please parents who lived through your achievements. Understanding why you demand perfection will change this. The result? Imagine yourself more relaxed, having fun, and avoiding the burnout so many perfectionists experience. Believe it or not, you'll actually perform *better*. Another benefit? Those who work with you will perform more productively when you're able to appreciate their efforts.

7. You have difficulty listening to people. Whether you mimicked an insensitive parent or rebelled against a parent or sibling who was needy and dependent on you, you can now become more responsive to others. Your new knowledge will help you squelch your assumption that everyone else in your life will become excessively dependent on you. The result? Others will see you as a caring person instead of an insensitive one.

8. You are excessively demanding of attention or of having your demands met. You now can start to see that you probably developed this quality as a rebellion against an insensitive, rejecting parent, and that you may be worried that the people you currently deal with will also be insensitive to you. The result? You'll pay more attention to other people's needs and you'll have more positive responses than antagonistic ones coming your way.

9. You have gotten into trouble by stealing or cheating. Whether you mimicked a dishonest parent, rebelled against a parent who took advantage of you, or behaved in unethical ways to make a parent feel morally superior, you are now in a position to use your knowledge to change this undesirable behavior before you ruin your life.

10. You give in too easily to requests, causing others to take advantage of you and to lose respect for you. Whether you submitted to a controlling parent, rescued a weak, needy parent, or mimicked a parent who always made concessions to others, you neglected your own interests for the interests of others. And you continue to do so. Now you have the tools to promote yourself and act more assertively. The result? You'll earn respect from others, and this will encourage you to continue on this new path.

Knowing the underlying causes of your self-defeating behaviors as you now do will make *correcting* any of the above patterns possible. Now when you get angry with yourself for behaving in ways you hate, you can say to yourself, "I know I'm doing this because I'm responding to a past behavior of someone in my family, but it doesn't mean that anyone in my *current* life requires it."

Changing and presenting yourself to others in a more constructive way will allow you to experience life in a more positive way. You'll stop making the same assumptions about other people that you did about your family. The conscious awareness of your dynamics will eventually overcome your self-defeating behavior.

What Advice Would You Give a Friend?

Imagine a friend coming to you for advice for the very same problems you are experiencing. What would you say? Chances are you'd force yourself to assess the situation objectively, not with the emotional responses that you made as a child and that you continue to make as an adult—at least until now. What would happen if you applied the advice you give your friend to yourself? For example, consider the advice you'd give a friend who told you his son refused to listen to anything he said. You might ask your friend, "Are you too critical? Are you bossy? Do you listen to your son?" Assessing your friend's attitude, in a calm and nonjudging manner will help you understand your own behavior toward your son and his refusal to listen to you. Now apply what you've learned to your own particular situation.

Problems with Relationships: The Split between Love and Sex

What's causing your problems in your personal life? Some of the same personality qualities that undermine your ambitions can also spoil your relationships. What about *accommodation?* Here's an example. If you feel responsible for rescuing everyone you think is unhappy, you may not be able to resist requests or demands made on you. The result? You'll feel angry with yourself for getting taken advantage of. Your dilemma is probably caused by having to make excessive sacrifices for a family member you felt sorry for.

Review your family profiles and look again at the chart titled "Checking Out Your Symptoms" above, and locate your problems with rescuing people. Once you examine your past and realize that a particular family member's unhappiness was not your fault, you'll realize that you deserve to do better for yourself. You've been released from psychological jail! In the future, every time you catch yourself acting too self-sacrificing toward someone, you'll be able to use your new knowledge to realize that you're repeating a pattern from your past that doesn't apply in your present.

What if you find yourself angry for not asserting yourself, yet you don't realize you're too worried about making the other person feel unhappy? What do you do? You let your anger be the signal that you've once again been too self-sacrificing. Then ask yourself, "Why am I doing this now?" Is your spouse or lover currently acting victimized?

Another way to help figure it out is to ask yourself, "If someone else, someone who was a rescuer like me, asked *me* what to do about his or her current self-sacrifice, how would I evaluate it and what advice would I give? Now apply the advice to your own situation.

What if you are a person who has affairs and you want to understand why? You want to be more intimate, but don't understand what's stopping you from achieving this. All you really know is that having affairs creates distance and means you never become too close to your lover *or* your spouse. Do you do this because your parent was rejecting? Now, in order to avoid rejection again, you keep yourself from getting too emotionally involved by having affairs. Or, instead, was your parent too possessive of you? Did that parent require the utmost devotion from you? Eventually, did you feel completely trapped? If so, your motivation for your many affairs is to never allow yourself to become trapped by obligation again. Knowing this now will help you distinguish between the trapped feeling you felt *then* due to your parent's need for you and the sincerest interest that your spouse or lover may have in you *now*. Do you see how recognizing the dynamic that applies to you can help you today? Once you do, you can really begin to think about and solve the motivations for your current problem behaviors.

It should be a relief for you to realize that some of your behaviors toward others (especially those behaviors you dislike) are not always provoked by their behavior toward you. Your new sense of self-knowledge makes it possible for you to improve your relationships with others.

Moving Ahead

I've presented a number of mechanisms that help explain how guilt and resentment are responsible for how people get stuck with behaviors they hate, and why it is so difficult to change. I've also presented you with a way of creating profiles for yourself and family members so that you can apply what you've learned. Next up you'll see how living your life in an attempt to please one parent may have caused you to displease the other. It's a maddening, wearisome, and confusing world that I call "double trouble," and knowing what you now know, it shouldn't come as a surprise to find our old "friends" guilt and resentment rearing their troublesome heads here, too. However, armed with the new self-knowledge found in your family profiles, you can say goodbye to them, just as you did in other self-defeating behaviors.

CHAPTER 12

Double Trouble in Your Family

WELCOME TO THE MIXED UP world of "double trouble"—a particular dilemma that occurs when your attempt to *accommodate* one parent's or sibling's shortcomings antagonizes, provokes, or disappoints the other parent. If one parent or sibling feels threatened by your success, whereas your other parent needs you to be successful in order to feel fulfilled, you've just entered the confusing and frustrating realm of "DT" or double trouble.

Chances are you're familiar with how "double trouble" emerges in divorces. Parents compete with one another for the affection of their children, with each parent hoping to be preferred. They do this to relieve the guilt they feel for being at fault in the family breakup. Sometimes, one parent wants to get even with the other by becoming the children's favorite while highlighting the failings of the other parent.

This makes it difficult for children to be close to either parent because they fear hurting or betraying the other one. If the children are young when the divorce occurs, they may learn to hold back their true feelings toward people, unconsciously fearing that closeness to one person is associated with disappointing someone else.

▨ LEE ▨

Lee was never going to make both happy. Lee, a forty-five-year-old woman, had been rejected by her cold mother as a child. Whenever Lee went to her for affection, comfort, and reassurance, she was turned away. Lee responded by *accommodating* and being self-reliant and independent. Now she wouldn't burden her mother by requiring comfort from her. As an adult Lee didn't feel comfortable turning to others for support because she thought that they'd feel burdened by her, just as her mother did.

Lee's parents were estranged from each other and slept in separate bedrooms. Lee's mother came from an upper-class family of "old money" and felt that her husband wasn't up to her social standards. Lee enjoyed spending time with her father, who was affectionate and emotionally available, and yet she wasn't completely at ease reciprocating his affection. She worried about being closer to him than her mother had been to him.

Because she was so independent and self-reliant, Lee attracted men who wound up depending upon her, taking her for granted, but not being emotionally supportive of her. When men were responsive to Lee, she had a hard time reciprocating their affection. She felt guilty (just as she had with her father) about having the kind of relationship with a man that her mother didn't have. She also worried about burdening them the way she had felt with her mother.

Lee's double trouble centered on the fact that when she was emotionally aloof, her mother approved and her father was unhappy. When she was affectionate and emotionally present, her father was happy but her mother wasn't. And so, aloofness and emotional responsiveness were waging a battle inside Lee, and with neither side able to win, Lee became the big loser in the "double trouble" war.

There are other ways in which people are forced to confront their complicated double trouble issues. In the

case of Robin, her double trouble came out in her struggle
for independence versus neediness.

ROBIN

Robin was a competent adult. A married business
executive, Robin came to me for help with depression. It
began just after her father's death, when she began
complaining about her husband, her job, and her weight.
At first glance, it seemed that Robin's problems stemmed
from the loss of her father. But that wasn't the case. Robin
was really feeling sorry for her lonely mother, who
compensated by becoming overinvolved with Robin's two
needy brothers. It was only when she was acting in a
mothering role that her mother felt fulfilled.

Robin, however, didn't need her mother, and she felt
guilty about that. "I don't need her. My life is not a mess."
Robin's father expected her and her younger sister to be
like him: punctual, responsible, and strong, and Robin
grew up feeling she could handle any problem presented to
her. Her mother, on the other hand, was weak and easily
dominated by Robin's father. He was contemptuous of his
wife's weakness. This in turn, served to reinforce in Robin
the importance of being capable and resilient. Here, then,
was Robin's double trouble: If she *accommodated* her
mother's need (by being weak and in need of her help), she
would disappoint her father. But if she managed her life
effectively, she'd make her father happy but deprive her
mother of having a maternal role in her life. This was a
classic double trouble dilemma.

What follows is a chart that highlights other examples
of double trouble.

EXAMPLES OF DOUBLE TROUBLE

Parent or Sibling A	Parent or Sibling B
Needs you to succeed to feel good. Lives through your accomplishments (in grades, sports, popularity, success with the opposite sex).	Is competitive with you and is threatened by your successes.
Is depressed and needy. You are overly attentive.	Feels neglected by your attention to the other parent.
Rejects you when you try to be close or want reassurance. You become independent and emotionally self-contained.	Is possessive and enjoys closeness. He or she feels hurt by your distancing.
Wants you to be independent and strong.	Wants to baby you.
Can't tolerate weakness.	Can't tolerate strength.
Prefers girls to boys. If you are a girl, you please this parent but not the other.	Prefers boys to girls. If you are a boy, you please this parent but not the other.
Is emotionally erratic or explosive, possibly because of heavy use of drugs or alcohol. You become excessively vigilant and worried all the time.	Feels upset or frustrated by your excessive worry and vigilance. ("Enough already.")
Is a failure, causing you to feel sorry for him or her.	Needs to be admired.

As in the other chapters where we've presented charts and you've worked hard to process them and integrate them into who you are today, the charts themselves serve as the Exercise for this chapter.

Moving Ahead

Congratulations, you've finished Part II. Hopefully you're beginning to have a better understanding of your mind-`sets, *and* maybe you're also starting to master them. As you move into Part III you'll see how the skills you've been acquiring and building can be applied in specific areas of your life.

The case studies that comprise a great deal of Part III are there for you to gain a deeper understanding of the information that we've set out in Parts I and II. Reading about the real-life situations of real people who have faced, and successfully dealt with, what you are now facing puts what we've been discussing in a different perspective by providing you with more of a world view. It also does something else that I feel is equally important. It reinforces something I said in the very beginning of the book: *Don't give up hope.* It is my wish that these case studies help to keep your hope very much alive.

PART III

SECRET SUCCESS CODES FOR WEIGHT LOSS, LOVE AND SEX, WEALTH, AND PARENTING

CHAPTER 13

Why Am I Fat and
Why Can't I Lose Weight?

HOW MANY TIMES HAVE YOU ushered in yet another New Year with a resolution to lose weight? How many times have those resolutions been realized? Why is it that with innumerable, well-publicized diet and exercise programs, personal trainers, self-help books and strategies, weight loss still eludes you? How come if you know that a healthy diet and regular exercise are necessary to shed pounds, your pounds don't shed? Why isn't the task of losing weight as easy, for instance, as learning and applying the information you get from a class on using a computer?

The problem has been that until now, the knowledge that you needed to lose weight was not found in books or classes. The information you need for successful weight loss is found by uncovering the cause of your self-defeating behavior. In the chart below you'll see the six underlying reasons why people continue to overeat in spite of their desire not to. One of the ways I want to make a confusing subject simple, understandable, and usable is to summarize different reasons for overeating. After reviewing the chart, I will present the real life stories of people who had different motivations for becoming fat and staying fat. They overcame the problem once they understood their hidden motivations.

You'll learn the importance of recognizing which of *your* family experiences set you up for failure, and, if your compulsive overeating or lack of motivation to exercise makes you miserable, you'll probably recognize your own pattern in the dynamics of one of the stories that follow. But first, let's recap how to read the chart: The left column shows how someone becomes fat to *accommodate* a parent who acts hurt or threatened by his or her child eating normally or being attractive. The middle column describes how one becomes fat as a result of *rebelling* against a parent's excessive behavior. The third column is about *mimicking* an obese parent or sibling. The stories that follow the chart will bring to life how the self-defeating pattern of overeating developed in real life situations. Do any of them apply to you? Read on.

▨   PAMELA   ▨

Pamela was feeling responsible for her mother's unhappiness. Pamela was a 24-year-old, overweight woman who came to see me because she was so distressed and frustrated by her compulsive overeating. She was pretty, bright, had a history of academic success, and was aware that her weight got in the way of her success with men. Pamela was *unaware* that she acted antagonistically toward men who were interested in her. By overly focusing on their negative qualities, she usually rejected them before getting to know them at a deeper level.

Pamela was not a wallflower, and she didn't lack men to date because *initially* she was engaging and lively, charming and at times flirtatious, and could carry on intellectually stimulating conversations. However, she did notice that it wasn't long before they stopped calling her. She assumed that it was due to her being overweight, because often her dates told her how attractive, even beautiful, she'd be if she lost weight (about forty pounds). This, however, was easier for her to swallow than the more painful recognition that it was her negative *attitude,* not

Accommodation **You are overweight in order to not hurt or threaten your parent or sibling.**	*Rebellion* **a. You rebel against your parent's hurtful expectations of you.** **b. You hope the parent will get the message and change his or her behavior.**	*Mimicking Their Deficiencies* **You feel it's wrong to be better off in attractiveness and normal weight than they are (especially if you feel that you had something to do with their plight).**
1. They are competitive with you about looks. They are insecure about their attractiveness and weight and jealous of those who are attractive. So you overeat.	1. Your parent is obsessed with thinness and your weight and eating habits. You rebel against the pressure of these demands on you by overeating.	You believe that their problem with weight resulted from your being a burden to them. Therefore you feel that you don't deserve to be better off than they, and you remain fat.
2. Your success with the opposite-sex parent makes your sibling or other parent feel left out. So you stay fat to not be favored and to protect the sibling or parent who's left out and not appreciated.	2. Your parent withheld food, especially desserts, as a way of manipulating or punishing you. You rebelled by secretly eating desserts whenever you could.	
3. Your parent feels especially happy when you eat heartily and enthusiastically. He or she likes plump kids, so you don't stop when you are full.	3. You weren't allowed certain foods because of allergies or illness, which caused you to feel cheated. You rebelled by overeating foods - that people say are bad for one's health.	
4. Your parent was very tight with money and couldn't stand for you to waste food. So you eat everything on your plate.		

her image, that was actually responsible for her
unfavorable dating outcomes.

An early evaluation showed that the cause of her
obesity was *not* a medical condition (like a low metabolic
rate). When I asked if any members of her family suffered
from weight problems, were excessively worried about
weight, or were preoccupied with no-fat foods or special
diets, she said "not at all." With no obvious explanation
for her difficulties with men, turning to her family
relationships to discover Pamela's unconscious motivations
became the next step. Pamela was extremely well treated
and loved by both of her parents. So what accounted
for her difficulties with weight? Over time, the picture
Pamela painted of her father came more clearly into view,
and as it did, other things about Pamela started to make
more sense.

As Pamela grew up, her father became more and
more uninterested in, and emotionally distanced from, her
mother. This family dynamic had a huge effect on Pamela
because while her father distanced himself from her
mother, he continued to remain loving, affectionate,
and sensitive to Pamela. Her mother was also loving and
affectionate with her, but she was clearly distressed about
the lack of attention from her husband, and she didn't
suffer quietly. Often, her mother cried and complained to
Pamela about her plight.

Pamela enjoyed her father's adoration, as any child
would, and she promoted it by being playful, funny,
and responsive to her father's affections. Because she
was successful with him, in contrast to her mother's
unhappiness, Pamela believed that she was responsible for
his lack of attention to her mother. One of the most
powerful childhood thoughts that emerged during her
therapy was, "If I'm beautiful, charming, and admired by

my father, it will cause my mother to feel left out, hurt, and jealous." This belief triggered strong, irrational feelings of guilt toward her mother. Irrational because her mother never accused Pamela of being responsible for her marital difficulties and never (overtly) acted jealous of Pamela's relationship with her father.

How did Pamela's guilt feelings toward her mother affect her life? She developed a false belief that she was responsible for her mother's unhappiness because she was attractive and charming. This evolved into a powerful, yet unconscious moral rule, "Being fat and unappealing is good." It was this deep-seated belief that undermined every attempt Pamela made to lose weight.

Pamela was wholly unaware that she thought this way, yet it caused the overweight pattern she hated in herself as an adult. Each time she dieted, her hidden guilt caused her to gain the unwanted pounds back. She unconsciously worried about making her mother, and by extension *all* women, feel hurt, unhappy, and envious of her attractiveness to men. The closer she got to her goal of being beautiful, the guiltier she felt, and the more she overate. Controlled by the mind-set "Being fat and unappealing is good," Pamela remained unable to do what was necessary to be appealing to men, as an accommodation to her mother's problem.

What would you think, as an adult, if one of your parents told you that he or she was divorcing the other because *you* were more attractive? Would you think that was absurd? Is it likely you'd accept blame for your parent's fault? Probably you wouldn't, and in much the same way, Pamela eventually realized that she had been falsely blaming herself for her mother's unhappiness. (Her parents' difficulties were not just independent of Pamela, they even preceded her birth.) As Pamela became more aware of the origin of her self-defeating behavior, she became more comfortable with being attractive to men. Not only did she lose weight, but she also stopped being negative with men who were interested in her.   ■

Rebellion's role in weight issues shows up in the next case study. Let's take a look at Allie, a young woman who wanted to establish her own rules for living and who instead established her own way of rebelling.

■   ALLIE   ■

Allie was resentful of her parents' control. Allie was another overweight client of mine. Raised by upper-class parents, Allie was required, especially by her father, to obey their rigid social standards. If she didn't she was strongly reprimanded. What *were* her family's social standards? To have proper social graces, play only with children of their class, adhere to their political outlook, and be athletic, thin, and beautiful.

As a child, Allie worried that her parents would feel betrayed and hurt if she made choices different from theirs. As a result, she was the perfect child. The moral rule Allie developed was "Living my own life and having my own values is a crime." If she did violate her rule, Allie would make her parents feel threatened. However, as Allie got older, she rebelled more and more against their control over her. This was Allie's response to resenting not having a life of her own.

To prove to herself that she *had* a separate identity, Allie began following her own rules. She stopped playing sports, dressed poorly, adopted contrary political views, socialized with people who'd have offended her parents, and she became overweight. What was the point of all this? What was Allie trying to gain from her behavior? First, she was communicating to them how distasteful their approach to her was, and second, she wanted them to be more accepting of her own choices. Ironically, Allie never actually developed her own independent ideas and values. She strictly adhered either to her parents' values or to those that were the exact opposite of them.

Overeating was how Allie maintained her uniqueness. She couldn't achieve her conscious goal to be healthy and attractive because it coincided with her parent's goals for her. One day, in our session together, Allie said, "If I lose weight I will feel like nothing." When I asked her why, Allie responded with, "I want to do what suits me and not be the way my parents want me to be." Is this the way a truly independent person would act? Allie thought so. She prided herself on her independence and more than once she boasted to me about it. One of those times, however, I challenged her. On that day I told her that I thought she was one of the *least* independent people I had ever met. Needless to say, Allie was completely startled by my comment. Asked what I meant, I pointed out to her that nothing she did was truly a reflection of her own free choice. She was still totally controlled by her parents' values and desires of her because she was doing exactly the opposite of what they wanted. And really, this was no different from behaving exactly according to their wishes. It was just approaching life from the back door of their values, rather than from the front door. If she were a truly independent person, she'd think about the decisions she was making in terms of whether or not they were things she really wanted to do, *not* whether they were things parents wanted her *not* to do.

Allie's first reaction to my comments was laughter, a derisive kind of laughter. After that passed, Allie grew quiet. She began to cry as she realized that she had been just as trapped by her own rebellious behavior as she had been by her parents' controlling behavior. She realized that for so long, all of the choices she had been making were self-defeating choices.

As sad as she was to discover her own truth, for Allie this was also a breakthrough. Gradually, from that point on she began to look at her actions by asking herself whether they served *her* interests or not. Together we worked at examining both sides of a choice she needed to make. The lingering struggle Allie had to deal with was the shock of arriving at a decision that was not only in *her* best interest but also happened to be something *her parents* would approve of too (like when she started losing weight). In these moments, Allie was still controlled by the danger of conforming to her parents' desires and of going in the opposite direction just to prove she wasn't a wimp. The process of evaluating both sides to discover what worked for *her own best interests* allowed Allie's self-destructive behavior to decrease. It also allowed her to become the independent person she wanted to be but never really was.

Think about the logic behind her thinking. As an adult, if your parents said that their life was ruined because you were not exactly like them, would you accept blame? No, you probably wouldn't, and probably comments like that wouldn't influence you to change your ways. But for a child, as we've seen, it is different. ■

Next we meet Pat. By choosing a dangerous lifestyle of binging and starving, she was mimicking her mother, and by doing so she hoped to relieve herself of the guilt she felt over hurting her mother.

▪ **PAT** ▪

Pat was trying to not be independent. Pat came to see me with complaints about her eating habits, which involved binging and starving herself. Pat would alternate between periods of being fat with periods of being excessively thin. Her father's eating habits were normal, but her mother's pattern with food alternated between binge eating and obesity, and starving herself. Our task was to discover why Pat followed her mother's unhealthy eating habits and not her father's more healthy ones.

Pat's mother's main satisfactions came from her overinvolvement in the decisions and life of her children. As a result, she made it difficult for them to become independent of her without experiencing guilt. What did that mean exactly in Pat's life? If she (and her siblings) tried to make decisions for themselves without their mother's input and control, their mother became upset and angry. And then what would she do? Begin binging on food. And how would Pat feel? Guilty. Pat's mother actually *told* her that she was hurt, and acted wounded by Pat's independence. She'd yell angrily that Pat "wasn't listening to her." She'd tell Pat she was "going to make a 'tragic' mistake." She'd warn her that she'd "regret her decision for the rest of her life." If Pat didn't take her advice, her mother would say, "How could you be so stupid? I can't believe that you wouldn't listen to me." And then, in an anguished tone, she'd scream, "I can't believe I gave birth to such an obstinate child!" As Pat's mother's agitation increased, so did her compulsive overeating.

You can easily see why Pat assumed that her mother's anguish over food and money was caused by Pat's desire to become independent of her. Her sense of guilt about being independent of her mother cemented Pat's new moral rule: "Independence is bad." Pat's rationale was, "If I become independent and make my own decisions, my mother will be hurt and feel that she has no purpose in life. That will cause her to either binge or starve, and become tight with money or overspend."

But why did Pat *mimic* her mother's out-of-control behavior? Why not identify with her father's attitudes about food and money? Because relief from guilt requires atonement and punishment, and one way to atone for hurting someone else is to be just like the person you hurt. If you experience the same problem that you think you caused in that person, you prevent yourself from being better than the person you hurt. Your self-imposed punishment has worked to relieve your guilt.

In Pat's situation, she mistakenly believed that her attempts at becoming independent caused her mother's eating problems. She felt guilty for hurting her mother in this way. This, in turn, made her feel that she *deserved to have the same eating problems that she had caused her mother to have.* By mimicking her mother, Pat was communicating that she was like her, and not independent of her. This is why Pat assumed her mother's eating problems rather than eat normally, like her father.

As an adult, what would you think if your mother told you that she binged when she ate to the point of obesity, alternating with starving herself, because you were making independent decisions. Wouldn't you think that was absurd? Is it likely you'd accept blame for those problems? Probably not. But as a child with limited experience, that's exactly what Pat inferred from her mother's problems. Like Pamela, she accepted blame and responsibility and acted in such ways as to try to alleviate the effects of her perceived misdeeds.

Pat's self-destructive message caused her to alternate between binge eating and starving herself. Her guilt feelings resulted from thinking "I hurt my mother by being independent of her or by being more like my father."

In the earlier profile, Pamela's self-destructive message caused her to avoid being attractive to men. Her guilty feeling resulted from her thinking, "I hurt women by making them feel envious of me." Both of these women acted automatically because of their false beliefs about the responsibility they assumed for hurting their mothers. ▪

Motivation: Feeling Sorry

What happens when your *normal* weight makes you feel guilty? If you grew up with an obese parent or sibling, the guilt that you are healthier or better off than that person could cause self-defeating behavior. You actually feel sorry for your obese parent or sibling, and so you remain overweight, in effect communicating that you feel sorry and he or she should not feel so bad because you are actually in the same boat.

Paul is someone who could never do enough for his mother. His struggles with his weight represent his very personal rebellion against her.

▪ PAUL ▪

Paul was fearful of being manipulated. Paul's chronic struggle with weight was influenced by his unconscious rebellion against having been manipulated by his mother. She withheld desserts from him when her guilt-provoking comments were insufficient to manipulate Paul into paying more attention to her than could be expected of any child. At the same time, she was never satisfied with the attention Paul gave her.

Whatever efforts he made on her behalf were never enough: If he got her flowers for her birthday, she'd ask if they were just a last-minute thought; when he called, she'd complain that it was too late in the day; if he visited, she'd say, "How come you didn't come over sooner?" Get the picture?

Paul, a very successful businessman at the top of his field, had studied and attended every weight-loss method known to man. But in spite of his vast knowledge about the subject, he was unable to successfully control his overeating. His physician had done everything possible to influence Paul to lose weight because of early but significant cardiac changes. He finally referred him to me.

What was unknown to Paul was that he subconsciously resented anyone, including his physician, who supported his weight-loss goals. He experienced that support not in a positive way, but instead as if they were attempting to take something of value away from him. You see, Paul had associated food as something to hold onto—especially snacks and sweets, because his mother withheld them to punish and manipulate him for not pleasing her. Therefore, when his weight-loss experts and his physician recommended that he give up desserts, he internally rebelled by defiantly overeating, as if it were his mother manipulating him.

Paul duplicated his childhood experience of rebelling against a mother who was impossible to please. He had no choice but to rebel—his mother was never happy with anything he did.

Over time, it became clear to him that he had confused weight loss with feeling deprived, and that he was responding by defiantly overindulging his sweet tooth. Within a year, he was able to gradually overcome his overeating. ◼

Eating to Please Parents

A bum walks up to a woman surrounded by her three plump children, and says, "Lady, I haven't eaten in three days." "Force yourself," she says. Another motivation for overeating is to please parents who derive special satisfaction from nourishing their children. It is the parent who says "Eat, eat—the children in China (or Africa) are starving." If the child is reluctant to stuff him- or herself, the parent becomes unhappy and frustrated and may say, "What's wrong with you?" or " How could you do this to me?" As a result, these children are reluctant to stop eating when full because they feel guilty about disappointing their parents' need for happiness. Again, this is a self-defeating accommodation to a parental flaw. The story about Sam is a good illustration of this.

▓ SAM ▓

Sam was seeking connection. He was a 55-year-old wealthy retired businessman who suffered from diabetes, obesity, high cholesterol, and high blood pressure. You would think that with all of these life-threatening conditions he'd be motivated to lose weight to improve his health and to get off medication.

But Sam had absolutely no idea what prevented him from solving his weight problem, and was also unaware of what in his eating habits was responsible for his difficulties. When he reviewed his meals, it seemed to him that his portions were reasonable and that he wasn't overdoing desserts. The source of the problem didn't emerge for some time, until he began to recall some of his childhood family circumstances.

When Sam was growing up his parents were estranged from each other for many years. There were continual parental battles because of severe personality differences, arguments about money, and his dad's affairs. His mother wasn't a slouch or pushover by any means. She was a strong-willed woman who readily complained about her husband's shortcomings directly to him, as well as out loud to anyone in her presence.

Sam's older brother, who had a critical nature and bad temper similar to his father's, was continually creating havoc at home and trouble in school. He was very impulsive, antisocial, and totally insensitive to his effect on others. His behavior was probably a rebellion against his domineering mother.

In contrast to his brother, Sam was for the most part congenial, easygoing, and soft-spoken. These qualities of accommodation enabled him to best survive the problems he faced with three very difficult family members. His mother sought him out because of his receptivity to her, and would frequently have conversations with him at night after everyone else had gone to bed. Sam was happy to have this connection with his mother, although he was also ambivalent about it because he sometimes felt burdened by his role as her confidant, and also because it generated intense jealousy from his brother.

What was most relevant to his current condition was that during those late-night conversations with his mother in years past, she would serve him warm milk and peanut butter sandwiches. His mother seemed so happy to see Sam enjoy her offerings of food, and this reinforced for him his ability to be instrumental in being the source of her only family satisfaction.

What Sam was totally unaware of was why he habitually made himself peanut butter and jelly sandwiches with warm milk before going to bed every night. This habit, which contributed strongly to his weight gain, gave him an ongoing symbolic connection with his elderly mother, whose only happy family relationship was with Sam. Every time Sam overate he unconsciously relived the historical intimacy with his mother when they had late-night conversations.

What prevented him from stopping his eating habit was his feeling of guilt about not being available for his mother, who depended on Sam for friendship. She lived in another state. It was as if, by continuing his late-night peanut-butter-sandwich-and-milk habit, he was letting his mother know that he was still thinking of her. In this way Sam accommodated to his mother's need for companionship from him. Once Sam became aware of the purpose of his late-night eating habit, he was able to overcome it and begin to successfully lose weight.

As we continue to use case studies to help us learn about our own eating issues, let's turn to Danielle, a woman whose motivation for her inability to lose weight centered on her inability to let go of the special place she held in her mother's life.

▓ DANIELLE ▓

Danielle was struggling to forge her own life. Danielle was a twenty-two-year-old, very large woman. Danielle, like Pamela, felt very sorry for her mother, Harriet, not because her mother was overweight (she was not), but because her mother had been oppressed and dominated by Danielle's grandmother. This had caused Danielle's mother to feel depressed and to become overly accommodating and self-sacrificing toward everyone in her family. Her depressed moods were made worse because she had difficulty communicating with Danielle's father, who was exceedingly quiet. Unlike Pamela's father, who clearly favored Pamela over her mother, Danielle's dad was equally quiet and unexpressive with both Danielle and her mother.

To compensate for her unhappiness, Danielle's mother had forged a special closeness with Danielle by confiding in her, spending as much time with her as possible, and needing to know everything Danielle was doing and thinking. Danielle didn't realize how emotionally dependent her mother was on her until she left home for an extended stay in San Francisco.

The beliefs responsible for her problem with weight weren't immediately obvious, but became more apparent as she struggled to separate from her mother. She felt obligated to frequently call her mother when she was away from home so that she could keep her mother informed of every aspect of her life. Danielle had developed the hidden belief that to not contact her every day deprived her mother of the only significant person in her life. As a result she felt guilty.

As she became more aware that she felt guilty about separating from her mother, she decided to move to San Francisco, become increasingly independent, and act more assertive with people. Yet her problem with weight remained unchanged until she recognized that it served to undermine success with men. A successful relationship would finally draw her away from her mother's orbit into one of her own. ▪

And then there's Max. His weight was going up out of guilt, but this time with a twist.

▪ MAX ▪

Max was living in the past. Max was gaining weight. He was also supposed to leave on a visit to see his mom, who didn't live in the same state. But recently Max had gotten very busy at work; many projects required his attention and he had to cancel his visit. Max's mother did *not* make him feel guilty about changing his plans, but Max felt guilty anyway. The way he lessened his guilt was by eating more. Why? Because as a kid Max was skinny. Eating more made his mother happier. So here he is, today, eating more as an adult to make her happy once again. Understanding this connection of his past to his present allowed Max to take control of his eating. He lost the weight he had put on and kept it off.

The Power of Self-Knowledge in Controlling Overeating

If Pamela, Allie, Pat, Paul, Sam, and Danielle tried losing weight by following the advice of a self-help book, or by pure willpower, would they have succeeded? Could they have overcome the hidden beliefs and new moral rules that were the foundation for their feelings of guilt or rebellion? All of them had great difficulty changing their self-defeating behavior *until* they understood the purpose of their underlying beliefs. Prior to acquiring this knowledge, they would make progress toward losing weight and then feel guilty about it and accommodate to the parent by overeating (Pamela, Sam, Danielle), or resent a parent's control and rebel against it by overeating (Allie, Paul), or mimic a parent's behavior so as not to offend (Pat). Guilt or resentment caused each of them to be diverted from his or her goal. However, once they learned about the hidden beliefs that were behind their actions, they all made progress. As they began to understand that their behavior was based on incorrect conclusions they had made as children (about the experiences in their families), they began to have more positive results with their weight loss. Once they had greater control over the feelings of guilt or resentment that were making them behave in ways they hated, they were able to succeed where previously they had failed.

When Food Is the Enemy: Anorexia and More

What about people who *under*eat? What motivates an anorexic? Many of the self-defeating mechanisms that apply to *over*eating are reversed with undereating. For example, parents who are obsessed with their children's weight, and associate beauty with thinness, act wounded, stressed, and threatened when they notice the slightest weight gain in their children, usually their daughters.

They show their hurt with comments like "How could you let yourself go?" "You look so disgusting," "When I see you eat, it makes me sick," "Why can't you look more like Jane?" They also reinforce this position by continually admiring the beauty of models and other ultra-thin public women. Get the picture?

When a girl is made to feel guilty enough, she'll feel that it's wrong to eat normally because it will hurt her parent. She will *accommodate* by being consumed with worries about weight, will constantly look at her shape in the mirror, weigh herself twice a day, and be preoccupied with starving herself as much as possible. This may compel her to become addicted to diet pills, laxatives, and diuretics; to compulsively exercise; and even to vomit after meals.

On the other hand, *rebellion* against parents who derive satisfaction from their child's eating can also play a role in anorexia. This child would simply refuse to give in to and gratify her parents' interest in seeing her eat. Instead, she would develop an antagonism to food. Parents who withhold desserts as punishment can lead to an aversion to desserts or other foods, and this can also be the motivation for some people to become excessively thin. If this is something that hits close to home for you, look over this next chart, "Anorexia and More," as well as Paula's story, to gain a new perspective on an equally problematic eating issue.

▨ PAULA ▨

Paula was through with being envied. Paula was an interesting, engaging, and complex young businesswoman who suffered from anorexia and seemingly unrelated difficulties with men. At twenty-seven years old and single, Paula came to me mainly because she was perplexed about her relationships with men. While she had a very easy time attracting men, she rarely was excited by those who were smitten by her sex appeal, intelligence, and outgoing personality. Paula complained that those who were caring and adoring of her she'd quickly lose interest in or provoke fights with. Worse to her was that she was sexually excited by men who were somewhat indifferent to and critical of her.

Initially, Paula didn't focus on her anorexia, even though in her adolescence she required hospitalization for several months to treat the most severe phase of her eating disorder. What seemed most troubling to her was her lack of success in falling in love in spite of her appeal to men.

Paula's family was made up of an older married sister, a businessman brother, a father who was an attorney, and her mother, who was a business consultant. Her mother, blunt, outspoken, and outrageous at times, was clearly the most dominant personality in the family. She acted victimized, wounded, and outraged if she didn't get her way. The same held true if she wasn't appreciated for her central role in the family, and if loyalty to her and her

ANOREXIA AND MORE

Accommodation
You are anorexic in order to not hurt your parent or sibling.

Your parent is obsessed with thinness. You associate beauty with thinness and never feel you can be thin enough.

You weren't allowed certain foods because of allergies or health problems. You avoid foods that are generally considered bad for one's health.

Certain foods, especially desserts, were withheld as punishment. When you feel undeserving, you deprive yourself of food.

Rebellion
You are anorexic in order to rebel and protest against a parent's or sibling's unreasonable expectations.

Your parent or sibling is competitive with you about weight and looks. You take the competition too seriously and become anorexic.

Your parent was overly fulfilled when you as a child ate heartily. You rebelled by refusing food.

They were very tight with money and couldn't stand for you to waste food. You rebelled by leaving your food on the plate.

Mimicking
You mimic an anorexic parent or sibling in order to not feel better off than they.

You felt that your parent's or sibling's anorexia was somehow connected with you. Therefore you don't feel deserving of having normal eating habits.

expectations was not shown. Paula's mother clearly lacked warm maternal instincts and compassion and primarily admired people who were rich.

Since concern about her image was of prime importance, Paula's mother was usually impeccably dressed and perfectly made up. Vanity motivated her to have more than one face-lift, and she was always concerned about her weight, complaining when she detected the slightest gain. To the outsider, her mother's personality excesses weren't obvious. Paula's mother was exceptionally adept and skilled in her social dealings with friends and associates. She avoided being perceived by others as obnoxious by combining charm, brazenness, and clowning. From the outsider's point of view, her personality was likeable and larger than life.

One result of her self-centeredness was that she competed with her daughters for her husband's attention. Whenever he was involved in discussions with his daughters, she diverted his attention to herself. Paula's sister rebelled against her mother's competitiveness by becoming promiscuous early on. By refusing to relinquish her interest in her father and other men, she showed her defiance. However, her mother didn't get the message. Instead it provoked intense conflicts between the two of them. Paula's sister had two failed marriages, and in her third, she incited fights with her husband by constantly belittling him. Often her mother promoted the fights, as if she were threatened by her daughter's success with her husband.

Paula's brother also rebelled against his mother's control, authority, and rejections by developing an antisocial stance. Additionally, he rebelled by performing badly in school. Although many of his difficulties resulted from hating to be disciplined by his father, it was his mother who was responsible for inciting his father against all the children. She did this by complaining about how she had been wronged by each of them during the day.

How did this family environment contribute to Paula's eating disorder and her difficulties with men? Paula was the youngest child. She was also the most agreeable and accommodating to her mother's need to feel special, important, and in control. This quality endeared her to her mother, and Paula became her favorite, her buddy. Because Paula was pretty, vivacious, athletic, and smart, she served as the perfect extension or reflection of her mother's ego. As a result, she experienced very little of the unpleasantness inflicted on her rebellious siblings. As long as she was there for her mother, her mother was there for her, and Paula thrived. But at a price.

Early in her adolescence, Paula began to become aware of the intense resentment her siblings felt toward her as the favorite child. They teased her with sarcastic barbs like "Here comes mama's favorite." In addition, Paula experienced unconscious guilt toward her mother because her interest in boys diminished her loyalty to her mother. Paula also worried that her mother would feel threatened if she were successful with boys because her mother always had been so openly competitive with her daughters for the attention of her husband.

Paula became increasingly thin. Her mother became frantic. Still, this had no effect on reversing the slide toward illness because anorexia served to relieve Paula's guilt toward her siblings. As long as she was impaired and her mother distressed, she didn't have to worry about being envied as the "golden child." Her anorexia provided a second benefit in that it sustained the bond between Paula and her mother because Paula wasn't in any condition to separate from her.

With the help of medication and therapy, Paula recovered, but remained in an ongoing battle with her eating disorder for many years. As long as she suffered this way, Paula felt she was protecting herself from the envy of her siblings.

Paula dealt with her guilt in other ways, too. One was through her loss of ambition; another was through difficulties with men. As long as she was unsuccessful with men and/or attracted to those who weren't desirable, there was little danger Paula would move out of her mother's influence or have more happiness with men than either her sister or her mother ever had. Paula falsely believed that her success with men would threaten her mother by upstaging her *and* by causing Paula to leave her. In this way, Paula *accommodated* her mother's flaws. But in alienating men by demeaning them, she was also *mimicking* the way her mother treated her father.

As she became increasingly clear in therapy about her hidden self-defeating motives, first in relation to her jealous siblings and later those related to her mother, Paula was able to solve most of her problems, including meeting and dating caring men. Ultimately, she married a desirable, loving man. Her eating disorder eventually gave way, but very slowly, because Paula needed to hang onto it as a way of placating her mother and siblings because of the guilt she felt over her successful marriage.

Exercise: Now It's Your Turn

Have you come to false conclusions about your own experiences? What conclusions have you drawn about your responsibilities for the faults and problems of your family members? Make a list, this time one that shows the faults, or, if you want, the *problems* of your family members. We'll call it "*Their Problems.*"

Make a second list and call it *"How I Pay."* This one is about the cost to *you* of their problems.

Taking some time now to answer those questions will further you along on your path of discovering what's going on in your subconscious mind, and that's a big step toward making long-lasting changes in your life.

Moving Ahead

The next chapter reveals how and why many people have great difficulty finding and keeping the right partner. Knowing what you now know, it shouldn't come as a surprise to find our old "friends" guilt and resentment rearing their troublesome heads in love and romance, too. However, armed with the self-knowledge you've been actively acquiring throughout this book, you can say goodbye to them in love, too, just as you did in other self-defeating behaviors.

CHAPTER 14

Why Can't I Fall in Love or Stay in Love?

LOVE IS A SUBJECT THAT stimulates incredible interest. Within all of us lives a fundamental desire to be successful in love. There are powerful motivations to succeed in a relationship in order to reproduce, pass on your genes, and successfully nurture the children who carry them. There are other powerful motivations too: companionship and deep, shared understanding that create the desire for a successful love relationship. The desire, need, and search for love is universal, and when found love sustains us through the hard times and enhances the good ones. But when we can't find love, or when we *do* find it and then lose it, over and over and over again, love becomes a source of struggle and pain.

All of the people in this chapter had problems when it came to love. Their stories were chosen to shed light, not just on their problems but also on how discovering what in their family history accounted for their problem. Knowing this, they were able to move out of their problems with, and into, love—sustained, deep, and committed love.

As with previous chapters, a chart—this one called "Why Can't I Fall in Love or Stay in Love?"—is designed to help simplify your understanding. The people and stories that follow are to help you be aware of similar problems that you may face in your own life. Let's begin with Haley, a woman who was unable to fulfill her ambition to achieve success with men.

WHY CAN'T I FALL IN LOVE OR STAY IN LOVE?

Accommodation You avoid a close relationship in order to not hurt or threaten your parent or sibling.	**Rebellion** You avoid closeness to rebel against your parent's or sibling's damaging expectations of you. You hope to send a message that changes his or her behavior.	**Mimicking** You mimic your parent's or sibling's flawed relationship in order to not be better off than him or her, especially if you think you were responsible for his or her plight.
Your parent is rejecting and burdened by your desire for closeness. So you stay distant from people.	Your parent is possessive of you and emotionally dependent on you. You avoid closeness to protect against becoming trapped by another's dependency on you.	Your parent has had many affairs. You follow suit.
Your parent or sibling is hurt by your success with the opposite-sex parent. To protect that parent or sibling from feeling envious of you, you fail in your relationships.	Your parent was overly moralistic and critical of sex. You rebel by being promiscuous.	Your parent is unable to have a serious long-term committed relationship as a result of being too cold, domineering, critical, a victim, or the like. You mimic his or her flaw.
Your parent lives vicariously through your sexual exploits. To not disappoint him or her, you continue to have many affairs.	Your parent is domineering and controlling. You rebel by avoiding intimacy to escape becoming dominated again.	Your parent is disdainful of the opposite sex. You accommodate to his or her view and act contemptuously toward the opposite sex.
Your parent is needy and pathetic. You become a rescuer and feel guilty about abandoning them and pursuing your own relationships. You feel obligated to rescue your partner.	Your parent needs for you to have a perfect relationship. For your parent, no one is good enough for you. You rebel by having many affairs or making bad choices.	Your parent chooses abusive partners. You feel uncomfortable about feeling better off. So you also choose abusive partners.

▓ HALEY ▓

Haley was comfortable limiting her goals. When Haley walked into my office for the first time, she avoided eye contact. She was plump but pretty, charming but shy, and extremely cautious. She was tentative and uncomfortable when attempting to talk to me. Haley dressed in unattractive baggy clothes, had an unflattering hairstyle, and wore no makeup. She was a twenty-five-year-old single businesswoman who had just completed her MBA, and sought help because she was unable to attract and establish relationships with desirable men.

In the first few months, Haley elaborated on how unsure she felt of herself. She told me, "I feel I can't have anything without believing that I am taking it away from somebody else. If I present my ideas, I think someone else will feel that they didn't have a chance." And so when she would say something favorable about herself, she'd immediately cancel it by saying something unfavorable. When having to guide or correct her co-workers, she'd offset her suggestions with compliments. In disagreements she'd defer to others, and when she made a suggestion she'd follow it up with comments like, "I'm not sure that was a good idea." There were, it seemed, nothing but faults that she could see in herself.

Haley once said, "Showing my intelligence hurts other people; therefore, I must hide my intelligence." I explained to her that she would have to learn to face her fear about demonstrating her competence, and not worry about feeling envied.

How does all of that tie in with this chapter's theme of love? Haley liked that I supported her ambition, and she was, in turn, encouraged to feel that I could also help her to overcome the troubled relationship with her boyfriend.

And so we turned our attention to why Haley chose a boyfriend who treated her badly in the first place.

Haley's live-in boyfriend, Dennis, was less educated than she, and had children from a former marriage who he expected Haley to take care of. He also expected her to be subservient to him *and* to pay for his share of the expenses. Haley complained about her boyfriend, yet she became irritable when I tried to explore more about the relationship, and in spite of her complaints about Dennis, Haley never considered ending their relationship.

After a few months of this, I asked Haley, point blank, why she continued to be involved with Dennis when her doubts and complaints about him nagged at her? For some reason, *this* time she responded with relief and began talking about leaving him and getting her own apartment. She said, "I guess if I did what I wanted to do, I would be showing up my mother and sister and proving that their lives are wasted." This was a huge statement and a huge moment of clarity for Haley. She went on to explain that neither her mother nor her sister was happy in their marriages, and that her mother never hid her unhappiness. "When Mother complained about Father, I often thought that she could have married someone else." With those words, Haley revealed one hidden belief that was responsible for her staying with Dennis, a man who made her unhappy. She was afraid of being happier than her mother and sister.

Haley described her mother as virtuous, moralistic, and saintly. Her mother acted superior to Haley's father and complained that he swore, drank beer with his buddies, was a nonbeliever, and was an unsophisticated buffoon. She played the role of a victim to her husband, which made Haley feel sorry for her. When I asked her what that was like for her, her anguish at describing the relationship with her mother was apparent.

"Mother was so moralistic and self-sacrificing. She would whine and complain that she worked such long hours, all for my benefit, and that I was unappreciative. She made me feel like I owed her and should be there for her. Otherwise, I'd feel guilty for not being there when she needed me."

Haley disliked her mother's "saintly" qualities. She remembered an incident in high school when her mother encouraged her to date a boy whom Haley saw as having almost no personality or spark. As a girl, Haley interpreted this as her mother not wanting her to have a man with a dynamic personality, preferring instead that she have the same kind of man Haley's mother had chosen for herself. "For some reason I felt it was hard to choose someone I liked if my mother didn't like him," Haley said. When I asked what had made a more favorable choice difficult for her, Haley said, "my mother's suffering."

The end result of feeling sorry for her mother was that Haley felt obligated to become involved with men her mother selected. This was also a way for Haley to stay close to her mother, and to make her mother feel needed by someone. By closing off her positive feelings for her father and by replacing them with the same disdain her mother felt, Haley found another way to please her mother. This way they would both be in the same boat—if her mother didn't have a positive relationship with her father, well then, neither would Haley.

Haley was afraid to have a better relationship with a man than her mother had. If she did, she'd feel guilty. To avoid guilt, Haley became involved with Dennis, a man she felt contemptuous of, just as her mother was contemptuous of her father. When I explained this to her, Haley said she'd never thought of this before, and with her new awareness came immediate and welcome relief.

As Haley became more attentive to her own self-interests, she ended her unhappy relationship with Dennis and also became more assertive at work. Haley had learned to confront the childhood beliefs that required that she limit her goals for her mother's sake. Once her fears were gone, she moved forward in life and thrived.

Haley changed enormously over time. She became more comfortable with her sexuality and with competing with other women. "I'm feeling very sexual and I'm having sexual fantasies about my male supervisor—I'm feeling competitive with my co-worker, Mary, for his attention." She also wanted to be admired by people of quality and not "the ordinary types like my mother and sister," a big departure from the Haley who felt bad when she outshone her mother, sister, and co-workers. Remember how inhibited and self-effacing she was at the beginning of therapy? What a change! At a party, she danced seductively with men and said, "I have a really shapely body and plan to get more clothes to show it off."

Two years after Haley ended treatment with me, I received a letter from her saying that she had married her boyfriend (not Dennis) and was very happy.

Let's move now to Dan, a man whose difficulties establishing close relationships with the opposite sex were different from Haley's.

DAN

Dan was caught in a circle of parental disappointment. A promising young lawyer, Dan came to see me because he was feeling despondent after being fired from his law firm. His supervisors told him he wasn't assertive enough on behalf of his clients and that he had trouble making decisions. Dan was smart and extremely capable and couldn't understand why he had trouble speaking out and promoting himself and his firm. And it wasn't just in his practice of law that his timid nature wreaked havoc in his life. In his love life Dan also revealed that he was having big problems, too, being unable to establish relationships with women.

Dan's father was a laborer who believed he had never realized his true abilities, and so he would inappropriately boast about himself to increase his sense of worth. Often he was quick to find fault with others and to put them down. When Dan expressed an opinion, his father would first find flaws in Dan's point of view, without letting him finish what he wanted to say, and then he'd pontificate on the subject as though he were an expert. When Dan's mother was present his behavior worsened. He acted competitively with Dan and behaved as if he were jealous of the attention and affection Dan received from his mother. When guests were in the house, the situation was equally bad for Dan. The response? Dan became subdued around his father, restrained his pride in his school achievements, and kept his opinions to himself. This was the way Dan learned to protect *his father* from feeling threatened by him. He *accommodated* his father's lack of self-worth.

Unlike his father, Dan's mother adored her son. She admired him and talked openly about how proud of him she felt. She enjoyed his intellectual abilities and academic achievements, and over the years their relationship involved many lively and interesting discussions. Naturally, Dan was happy about his mother's love and admiration, but worried that her self-esteem and happiness were tied to his involvement with her as well as his intellectual accomplishments.

And so, the reasons for Dan's difficulty in making decisions became apparent. When he enjoyed his mother's pride in him for being bright and accomplished, he unintentionally threatened his father's self-esteem, causing his father to feel jealous. When he *accommodated* his father by acting subdued and keeping his opinions to himself, he disappointed his mother, who enjoyed him when he was lively and interesting to talk to.

Dan was caught in a psychological conflict, and his response to this struggle was to become ambivalent. Every choice had to be judged by whether it hurt his mother or whether it hurt his father, and so Dan alternated between shining and being subdued. The result, at the point in his life when he came to see me? Dan's adult life was characterized by the same indecisiveness that began in his childhood.

Indecisiveness undermined his effectiveness in law. His clients felt they lacked a strong advocate, lost confidence in him, and communicated their dissatisfaction to his partners. When it came to communicating his intellectual abilities *within* the firm, Dan faired no better. He constantly held back from demonstrating his intellectual ability, something he'd mastered from a childhood spent not wanting to make his father jealous and which he now applied in his adult life.

When it came to pursuing women he was attracted to, Dan became anxious to the point of being nearly mute. The reason? Success with women caused him to feel that he was disappointing *both* parents. Can you see why? Let's start with Dan's father. He was actually threatened whenever Dan's mother paid attention to Dan, which made Dan feel guilty. That guilt made Dan anxious about succeeding with women. As time went on in our work together, Dan understood that his fear of initiating conversations with women was based on his unconscious worry: If he succeeded in talking with women, he would make his father jealous.

As for Dan's mother? What place did she play in Dan's problems with love? Although she'd always been supportive of his accomplishments, Dan believed he was providing her with the companionship and stimulation her marriage failed to provide her with. *Unconsciously,* Dan believed that if he developed a close relationship with a woman, he wouldn't be available to his mother anymore and he'd disappoint her.

One more thing was holding Dan back from succeeding with women. He worried that once he was in a serious relationship with a woman, she'd become as emotionally dependent on him as his mother had been. He feared (unconsciously) being trapped by his own obligation to keep her happy and not disappoint her. The result? Dan protected himself by selecting women he knew didn't meet his criteria for marriage so that he wouldn't have to worry about falling in love and feeling trapped by the obligation to care for them.

When it came to sex, Dan had troubles there too. He finally met a woman who met his criteria for a serious relationship. She was attractive, educated, *and* independent. Obviously, her independence was a big part of it for Dan, who didn't want to have to worry that she'd become dependent upon him like his mother was. And so, it all sounded good with Dan's new girlfriend, Roberta. However, the first time they went to bed, Dan was impotent. Dan was extremely upset by his lack of performance, and not only because of his pride. Mainly,

Dan feared disappointing Roberta. Fortunately for Dan, Roberta was relaxed, and not at all disappointed. The effect on Dan was as positive as it was powerful. Over time, Dan became less worried about hurting and disappointing Roberta, and so his sex life with her became less strained and more satisfying.

As Dan became more aware of his anxiety about disappointing women who became dependent upon him, and also more aware of his worry about his father feeling threatened by Dan's success in life, both his professional life *and* love life improved dramatically.   ■

In the next story, a highly successful man, Duke, is pursued by many women but is unable to develop a loving relationship with any of them.

■ DUKE ■

Duke was seeing love as an obligation. Duke was a fifty-year-old man with many talents and accomplishments and wealth, who could solve almost any problem—except how to fall in love with one of the many desirable women who were attracted to or involved with him. The result was that Duke became a man of many marriages and many affairs. He liked bragging that a lot of men he knew were jealous of the amazing women that had fallen for him over the years. Yet, at the same time, his loudest complaint about his life was his inability to fall in love with any of them.

Duke was on the way out of his fourth marriage when he came to see me. Though he was feeling a tiny bit guilty toward his current wife, he wasn't really deeply affected by this, the latest of his many exits. As he recounted his numerous affairs and conquests, he recalled recently running into a very successful woman lawyer he'd first met thirty years ago. As he described this woman, it became apparent that he admired her very much. He told me that in order to marry a woman like that, a woman of such high caliber, he'd have to have been more adult, much more honest and less egocentric than he was. "If I had been different, such a woman would have been with me because she chose to be with me, not because of my money. This woman was special—she was self-sufficient and not needy like the others." It was at that precise moment that Duke experienced a painful realization. In a quiet, dispirited tone, Duke told me he'd been attracting women who wanted his wealth and power. He married women beneath his level and always with unhappy results. Duke was on top of the business world, but inside, he was miserable and lonely.

Duke told me that he lived a "life of deception." In his words, "I present an image to the world of fancy cars, big houses, elaborate trips, being in the limelight, and associating with famous people." But, he went on to explain, this image really represented his *mother's superficial values,* not necessarily his own.

From childhood on, his mother's fulfillment came through Duke's achievements. To keep her happy, Duke *accommodated* his mother's values and pursued a life of glamour, fame, wealth, and power. He even incorporated the same disdain for his father that his mother had voiced for years. Duke's father was a sweet, disorganized daydreamer with no common sense. Unlike Dan's competitive father, Duke's father supported his son. Duke felt guilty toward his father because his mother continually compared his successes with his father's failures. Duke was caught in a struggle between his mother's negative view of his father and his own true, positive feelings for his father—but his mother's attitude prevailed. And so Duke accepted her values for living and her conclusions about his father.

The childhood impact of his mother was still influencing Duke's professional behavior and making him miserable. Although he felt powerful, confident, and full of himself on the professional front, he would often present himself as tentative, overly modest, worried, and gloomy. Doing this made Duke feel less anxious; as he explained it, "I don't know if I want to be perceived as a peacock or a sparrow." When he was a "peacock," he became a magnet for needy, dependent types. These women, looking for rescue or to share in the glamour of his life, left him feeling lonely and empty inside. When he was a "sparrow," keeping a low profile, he knew he'd be disappointing his mother's expectations.

How did he deal with this dilemma? Duke adamantly demanded control over everyone in his life. He bragged about not having a boss for twenty-five years and said, "I can't stand being told what to do. I refuse to do anything unless it's my way—when I was a kid I demanded to get my way and my mother indulged me." Duke feared being controlled because he had been controlled by his mother as a child. He knew what it felt like, he knew it didn't feel good, and he knew he wouldn't let it happen again. Duke maintained control by creating a life of power, fame, material pleasures, and showmanship. This pleased his mother. But he never believed that anyone truly cared for him.

Duke rarely pursued women. He would, however, respond aggressively whenever a woman (single or married) showed any interest in him. Why did he do this, despite his conscious desire to *not* have a woman become dependent on him? The answer was simple. Duke didn't want to disappoint any of them. "I have always had this sense of responsibility to take care of women and make them happy," he said, then added, "What a tremendous burden it has been for me to keep them going." That was how he felt, he told me, with his mother, whose identity revolved around him. "Her life was me." At that moment he recalled the most relaxed time in his life. It was when he had retired from the fast track he'd been on and instead changed to a casual, rural lifestyle. During that time, what was so special for him was his freedom from having anyone dependent on him.

In a healthy relationship, a person doesn't feel burdened about making a spouse or partner feel happy. In a healthy relationship, a person feels free to say no. In a healthy relationship, a person feels comfortable about giving and receiving love. For Duke, none of that was possible in his relationships. For him, a relationship was a one-way street. For him, the whole burden of being the caretaker and fulfilling all needs was on him. When a woman responded to him, it made Duke feel even more obligated to care for her, and so he could never be comfortable in a relationship.

This helps us understand why Duke was a man of many marriages and affairs. He controlled women and kept emotionally distant from them because he worried they'd manipulate him. When a woman *did* become dependent on him, Duke would leave her. This was done to avoid the danger of sacrificing himself to her needs. The reason for all of his affairs can be explained in the same way. Duke would love them but leave them when they started to fall in love. This was because he associated a woman's love with an obligation to take care of her. Since he had difficulty saying "no" to women, he knew that their dependency on him would be at his expense. The result? Duke couldn't see any benefit to being loved.

Duke was adamant about not having anyone depend upon him, and so, for a time, he refused the requests of women he dated. But the more he understood about the source of his problem, the easier it became for him to be less anxious about rescuing women. Over time his new sense of control made it more comfortable for him to develop a close relationship with an intelligent, very accomplished, independent career woman. Ultimately, this relationship led to a moderately successful marriage.

Duke told me how good it felt to finally be involved with someone who didn't need to depend on him because she herself was self-sufficient (and interesting.) At the same time, he felt reassured about not being taken advantage of; her sensitivity and care for him was sincere. Duke's understanding of that meant that he had finally come to distinguish between his experiences with his mother and his new wife. ■

It's time to turn our attention to Caroline, an exceptionally bright and accomplished businesswoman who could outthink and outperform almost any man in the business world but was unable to use any of her talents to get a man for herself.

■ **CAROLINE** ■

Caroline was not about to imagine happily ever after. Consumed by her love of work, for years Caroline turned away from any desirable man who pursued her. Instead she got involved with emotionally distant men who did nothing for her. She told me, "When I have sex, I feel that I have to lie there and take it like I was being forced."

She was the youngest of three and, according to her mother, the best child and the best behaved. It was quite easy for her to achieve this status in her mother's eyes because of the rebellious behavior of her siblings—her sister was promiscuous and her brother abused drugs. Her siblings resented Caroline because they saw her as being too perfect—a "goody-two-shoes." Besides being well behaved, Caroline was also very responsive to her mother's needs. In short, Caroline was the perfect daughter.

When Caroline was eight, her mother divorced her father, who had become distant and cold toward his wife. It later came out that he also had been having affairs with other women. Caroline's mother became bitter and unhappy, causing Caroline to feel deeply sorry for her. Increasingly, Caroline made herself available to her mother in order to "be there for her." At one point she recalled how she'd be sick to avoid school and stay home "for Mother's sake." "I've always been able to figure out what people want and need and then do it. So I couldn't relax and be creative or focus on myself—I couldn't find what I wanted."

When she began to date, if Caroline talked about her boyfriends, her mother would criticize them. Caroline told me, "Mother was very possessive and jealous of my relationships. Her possessiveness makes you feel that you need to be her lover, and that you can't choose to be with anyone else." After some time in therapy, she wondered "if it is hard for me to feel loved by men out of loyalty to Mom." The possibility that this *accommodation* to her mother explained her difficulties with men was exciting to Caroline. The other reason for her difficulties with men was also connected to her mother, but in a different way.

What was it her mother drilled into Caroline's mind? The importance of work and self-reliance. What was it she *didn't* mention at all? Marriage and children. Why? "Because a man will disappoint you or die on you." Her mother's open contempt for women who didn't work led to comments like, "Any woman who is successful with men and has children is vapid." It's not surprising that in trying to please her mother, Caroline selected men who weren't emotionally available and chose instead to work compulsively in her career. Caroline pleased and *accommodated* her mother by adopting her mother's values for living.

Caroline became romantically involved with John, and she had no other way to describe him but as being a "good guy." Not only was he caring, reliable, bright, and successful, but best of all, he was in love with her and not married. As her involvement with him deepened, she began to become moody and self-critical. Instead of feeling excited and uplifted, her romance with John was creating bad moods and negative thoughts.

Caroline felt she was weak for fantasizing about marriage. "Mother hates that I'm becoming dependent on a man. It was very important to her that I be a big success, especially in a man's world." And how did Caroline relieve her guilt toward her mother who was contemptuous of romance? By having negative thoughts and being in bad moods about John. Realizing this, she immediately became more optimistic about John and her bleak mood lifted. Still, Caroline couldn't allow herself to contemplate a happy ending with John. If she was happy, she worried he'd leave her or something terrible would happen to end her happiness. If they were having problems, she was convinced they would never work them out.

Where did her inability to imagine a happy ending with John come from? You've got it: from Mom. Caroline remembered that her mother could *never* resolve her problems with her father; she understood where her pessimism with John came from. Caroline felt sorry for her mother. *Mimicking* her mother's difficulties unconsciously

put Caroline in the same boat with men as her mother had
been in with her father. In this way, she didn't have to
worry about outdoing her mother.

The more aware she became of her mother's influence
on her relationships with men, the easier it became for
Caroline to feel happier with John and to deepen her
relationship with him. However, Caroline still found it
difficult to have consistently positive feelings for him.
When John was unhappy, Caroline told me that she
believed that he would leave her. Was she to blame for his
bad mood? Caroline said she wasn't. What, then, made her
assume that it was her fault? Laughing, she said, "I know,
I just can't believe that it's okay for me to think that things
will work out with John when something is not right with
him, because my mother had such a different experience
with my dad."

Continuing to fall in love with John meant continuing
to become aware of her family history and how it created
roadblocks to their love. "The more attractive I became to
men, the less connected I was to my mother. I remember
enjoying my sexuality and then felt so guilty about it that I
played it down as much as I could." I reminded her that at
the beginning of therapy, she had said that when she had
sex she felt she had to lie there and take it. She replied,
"Mother hated men and favored girls. She said men were
bad, that they were evil, so if I like them it pointed out
what she didn't have."

Caroline began to reveal another negative influence
on her long-standing difficulties with men. As a result of
needing to be her mother's emotional caretaker, she had
developed hidden resentment about always having to be in
control, to take care of things when her mother was
nervous or unhappy. When John acted loving and
emotional, Caroline misconstrued it as neediness. Instead

of feeling delighted, she said she "felt disdainful toward him, as I do with my mother when she can't handle things." This created an unfortunate dilemma—when John needed her, she felt burdened and resentful, and when she needed him, she felt guilty because she was supposed to be totally self-reliant.

Caroline took the dilemma even further: "If men do things for me, I see them as weak. But if I do things for them, I resent them." Her continued awareness of how these feelings affected her increasingly freed her to become more romantic and more sexual with John. She began to stand up for herself with John against the negative effects of her mother's hatred for men.

Caroline and John eventually got married; one year later they had a child. ▪

Next we'll look at Sarah, a successful business consultant trapped in an abusive relationship.

▪ **SARAH** ▪

Sarah was afraid to hurt every person in her life. Sarah was given my name by a mutual acquaintance and called me because she wanted my advice about a female client whom she described as hopelessly trapped in an abusive relationship. Sarah wanted to know what could possibly make someone stay in such a miserable situation. I mentioned that there might be several causes, and that one of them could be the influence of growing up with a parent who had been abused. Sarah said that she found that "very interesting." The next day, she called me again, confessed that she'd actually been describing herself, and made an appointment with me for later that week.

Sarah was an attractive thirty-five-year-old woman

who was embarrassed to admit that she was in a serious relationship with an emotionally abusive man. And not for the first time, either. Four years previously, she had called off her engagement to another abusive man. However, before that relationship, Sarah had never been mistreated by a man.

For the past three years, Sarah had been living with Don and had tolerated a great deal of mistreatment from him. Don enjoyed finding a person's weakness and using it to dominate and take advantage of the person. He demeaned her physical appearance, her clothing, the way she interacted with other people. No matter what she did sexually, she never pleased him. And even though he was a very successful businessman, Don expected her to pay most of their living expenses. Sarah felt beaten down and humiliated, and vowed (repeatedly) to leave him. But she never did. Sarah came to me to try to understand why. *Why* was she with him and *why* wasn't she able to leave him?

When describing herself, Sarah used words like "aggressive," "successful," "tough negotiator," and "fighter for her clients." This description caused her to add another "why" to her list: *Why* could she be so strong for her clients but not for her herself?

After several meetings, Sarah mentioned that when her frustration with Don became so great that she threatened to leave him, he'd break down, get emotional, and promise to change. Sometimes, he'd even cry to the point of sobbing. When he did that, it made Sarah feel sorry for him and realize that he was actually very vulnerable.

Was she staying with Don because she was afraid of hurting him if she left? "Yes," that was exactly how she felt, adding "Don is very afraid of my strength." A month later her comment was, "He's walking wounded. I've been his strength. I think I'm so afraid of hurting him that I put myself in the position to be hurt by him instead." It was then that Sarah realized that feeling sorry for Don and making herself out to be a victim was her way of *accommodating* to Don's weakness.

Aside from playing the victim to the main man in her life, Sarah noticed that she was afraid to enter into relationships with appropriate men because she feared that they would fall in love with her and be hurt by her strength. She wondered if she was attracted to Don because initially he seemed strong and invulnerable to her—it was only later, when the relationship became serious, that she sensed vulnerability in him. Where did all of this start? Let's look at what Sarah's childhood was like.

Sarah was seven when her mother left her father because of his abusive behavior. Sarah later learned that her father became abusive only after he discovered that her mother had slept with other men during their marriage. Sarah went to live with her mother and new stepfather. It was here that she witnessed the physical abuse her mother suffered, having married a man who beat her regularly. During that terrible time, Sarah couldn't help but contrast the beatings her mother suffered with the attention she herself received from her stepfather. The stepfather, who was so cruel to her mother, flirted with Sarah and seemed to prefer her company. She feared hurting her mother if she accepted her stepfather's attention and gifts. A few years later, the marriage ended, her mother took up with a series of men, and Sarah went to live with her real father.

Sarah's father wanted to play the primary role in her life. He was strict, controlling, and extremely possessive of her and a disciplinarian who kept her from watching TV or dating. When she became seriously involved with her college boyfriend, Martin, her father acted jealous.

After Sarah grew up and left home, her mother reentered her life. Her mother, whom Sarah described as a magnet for men, was a very attractive, manipulative, sexy woman. She was very socially adept. But she was also a person without a core, and like a parasite, which lacks its own internal resources, she lived off men until they got fed up with being exploited and dumped her. Between men, Sarah's mother became pathetically needy, and would have emotional fits because she was alone.

Whenever her mother was between men, she would stay with Sarah until Sarah could no longer tolerate being drained by her mother's constant emotional need. During those times, Sarah remembered her mother as an emotional cripple who leaned on her and dragged her down.

Sarah said, "I provided my mother's strength. She made me feel that I was only thing she had. When I left my mother to make my own life, she fell apart. I felt guilty for abandoning her."

Sarah was deeply in love with her fiancé, Martin, a wonderful man whom she admired and who would never think of abusing a woman. Yet, in spite of being deeply in love with him, Sarah suddenly and unexpectedly ended her engagement to him without having any idea why. As she talked about how much Martin's love meant to her, she broke down and sobbed. Sarah looked back on that decision as the greatest mistake of her life.

One by one the reasons why her emotional history played a part with her boyfriend, Don, became clear.

- She had a better relationship with her father and step-father than did her mother (who had been abused), causing her to feel sorry for her mother.
- When she left her needy mother, her mother fell apart.

- When Sarah became increasingly educated, self-reliant, and independent, her father acted threatened because she no longer needed him to be her guide and her consultant in life.
- When she became engaged to Martin, her father became even more estranged from her because he felt displaced by Martin.
- When she unexpectedly left her fiancé, Martin, he was devastated.
- When she threatened to leave her abusive boyfriend, Don, he acted vulnerable and hurt.

Every experience just described resulted in Sarah's feeling terrible guilt toward her father, her mother, her fiancé, and finally, her current boyfriend. She felt that she had hurt all of them in some way. What did she do with all this guilt? First, she punished herself by becoming involved with Don, and then she continued to punish herself by staying in an abusive relationship with him.

And the truth is, Sarah had a hard time standing up for herself, not just with Don, but also in every aspect of her life. Because of her past, she was afraid of hurting *everyone*.

After several months of therapy Sarah embarrassedly confessed that for many years she had experienced sexual fantasies of being beaten and sometimes tortured by an older man. She would masturbate to these fantasies and used these thoughts to become excited during sex. It didn't matter whether sex was with a nice or an abusive man. Sarah mentioned to me that in recent weeks she had been masturbating more frequently to these same kinds of fantasies. Sarah was perplexed, thought about it more, and wondered if it had something to do with her increasing resolve to finally leave Don. Don sensed her determination and was responding by becoming increasingly needy and upset. I explained that when Sarah imagined herself hurt through beatings, it relieved her guilt about hurting not just Don but her mother and all the men in her past. Not only was she the victim, but she also elevated the man in the fantasy to the role of the strong, cruel one.

I explained that the older man who performed the beatings represented her father, who had been hurt by her strength and independence from him, and who felt jealous and displaced by her interest in boys, especially her love for Martin. The punishment fantasy relieved her feelings of guilt regarding her father, freeing her to enjoy sex.

Finally, Sarah's beating fantasies served another purpose for her: They helped to reduce Sarah's guilt toward her mother. Sarah's stepfather, you'll remember, had beaten her mother while being, in contrast, flirtatious and pleasant toward Sarah.

Sarah soon understood that her fantasy beatings were a way of *mimicking* her mother's suffering. When she realized that she was using them as a way to reassure her mother that she was no better off than her mother, Sarah was able to begin moving forward in her relationships with men. ▪

Let's switch from our case studies for a moment. We've been trying, in this chapter, to get a handle on why many of us have such a hard time falling in love, being in love, and staying in love. The use of fighting is one reason that, for some of us, love is always elusive.

Fighting in Order to Love

There are those of us out there for whom fighting makes it possible to feel safer about the dangers of closeness. What are these dangers?

Danger #1.   Intimacy equals obligation. This is an obligation to please a partner so as not to disappoint the partner. The more you fight, the more you're freed from the obligation to please.

Danger #2.   Loving too strongly equals fear of rejection or being taken advantage of. Fighting with your partner means that you can control how close you allow yourself to feel to that person.

Danger #3.   A happy relationship equals something you don't deserve. Fighting with your partner helps you deny that you are satisfied with the relationship, and in that way relieve your guilt.

Danger #4.   That your partner is weak and loves you too much equals your guilty knowledge that you can hurt, dominate, or reject the person. Provoking your partner into a fight means feeling reassured that he or she is tough, strong, and resilient.

If you know that you are a person who needs to fight to love, perhaps being aware of the above four dangers helps you better understand why the need to fight exists. For some, fighting isn't what they use in order to love, but fantasies are.

Pain and Pleasure, Pleasure and Pain

An observation was often made in the Soviet Union to describe how its communist economic system performed: The workers pretend to work and the government pretends to pay them. How does this apply to the sexual fantasies I have described, and some of the roles that people assume in their sexual play?

USING SEXUAL FANTASIES TO DEAL WITH FAMILY CONFLICT

Your Parent's Flaw	The Sexual Fantasy that Serves Accommodation	The Sexual Fantasy that Serves Rebellion and Mimicking	The Sexual Fantasy that Serves Mimicking
Authoritarian, abusive, and controlling parents require you to be obedient, to quash your independence, and may abuse you.	In your fantasy you become a sexual slave to someone else, and you may submit yourself to physical abuse.	In your fantasy you refuse to submit and instead you enslave and abuse your partner.	In your fantasy you enslave, control, and abuse your partner.
Weak and needy parents require rescue.	You have fantasies of sex with your parent or a parent substitute as a way of taking care of them.	You watch others suffer and ignore their suffering.	
Rejecting parents can't tolerate your being emotionally dependent on them.	In your fantasy you stay emotionally detached during sex. Instead of participating, you may prefer to watch others perform sexually.	In your fantasy you are outlandish to gain attention, and imagine your parent or others pursuing you sexually.	In your fantasy you rebuff your partner's advances.
Possessive parents require you to be devoted to them.	In your fantasy you are a sexual slave to the possessive parent or others, stimulating him or her to great sexual satisfaction. If your possessive parent is of the same sex, you will have homosexual fantasies.	In your fantasy you have multiple partners to protect yourself against feeling trapped by the obligation to one person. If you imagine your partner having sex with others, he or she will seem less possessive of you.	In your fantasy you require your partner to be slavishly devoted to your sexual desires.

USING SEXUAL FANTASIES TO DEAL WITH FAMILY CONFLICT (continued)

Your Parent's Flaw	The Sexual Fantasy that Serves Accommodation	The Sexual Fantasy that Serves Rebellion and Mimicking	The Sexual Fantasy that Serves Mimicking
Parents who live through your accomplishments require you to be perfect.	In your fantasy you are the celebrated sexual performer, arousing your partners to the greatest, most blissful ecstasy possible.	In your fantasy you are a sexual failure, humiliated, and degraded.	In your fantasy you require your partner to be the celebrated performer.

When describing sadomasochistic fantasies or role-playing, there is a similar mechanism at work. The person with the sexual masochist fantasy or role pretends not to inflict pain on others, past or present, by taking the role of the victim. ("Who me? I haven't done anything to inflict pain on anyone. I'm innocent. I'm the one who is suffering. I've been punished, I've paid my debt, so I am now free to have pleasure.") The sadist pretends to *not* be vulnerable, by inflicting pain and watching someone else suffer what he or she experienced as a child. In this way sadists distance themselves from the memories of their childhood suffering. In Sarah's case, she imagined herself as a victim in her sexual fantasies, but she also became a victim of Don's mistreatment.

The chart "Using Sexual Fantasies to Deal with Family Conflict" describes the types of fantasies people use to relieve their guilt about causing pain to their flawed parent, or to rebel against the excessive and destructive behaviors of their parents and siblings.

Moving Ahead

As we said earlier, the charts you've gone over and worked on in this chapter serve as the exercise, so you'll find no formal "Now Look at Yourself" here. In Chapter 15 we'll look at why success and wealth are so hard for some of us to achieve in our lives.

Why Do Success and Wealth Pass Me By?

ARE YOU FRUSTRATED BECAUSE YOU haven't been able to achieve your academic, financial, or career goals? Are you still losing money in the stock market? Ignoring the advice that you paid for? Selling when you ought to be buying, never taking your profits in time, selecting losing stocks, or confusing investing with gambling?

Are you wondering why you haven't moved up in your company? Do you have a tendency to alienate superiors or co-workers? Do you get fired from job after job? Are your relationships with employees, partners, or customers contentious? Do you assume it's everyone else's fault, never your own?

Two types of self-defeating motivations are responsible for most of the failures described above. Type One is based on specific family factors: You limit your goals as a way of pleasing *(accommodating)* a parent or sibling who resents your successes; or you *rebel* against the pressures to be perfect from a parent who lives through your accomplishments. Type Two is a result of your negative personality qualities, which interfere with your ability to relate well to people.

Look at the chart called "Why Do Wealth and Success Pass Me By?" and try to learn which examples apply to you. The first column describes how *accommodation* can cause failures with career, success, and money. The second column describes how *rebelling* against a parent's or sibling's excessive expectations cause you to undermine you goals. The third

197

WHY DO WEALTH AND SUCCESS PASS ME BY?

Your parent's and sibling's flaws	Your *accommodation* of their flaws inhibits your success	Your *rebellion* against their expectations of you causes you to fail	You *mimic* their failures because you feel sorry for them or responsible for their failings
They are jealous of people who are successful and wealthy. They may falsely boast to inflate their own achievements and demean you or others.	You help them to feel more secure by diminishing your successes or by being extremely modest.	You boast about or inflate your achievements.	You demean others and try to inflate your worth.
They failed in business, or gambled with investments, and lost large amounts of money.	You advise them how to be more successful and rescue people who have trouble succeeding. You may also limit your own successes.	You become so conservative that you are unable to invest creatively or start a business. Or you boast about your wealth.	You gamble or make risky investments and mimic their risk taking.
They are authoritarian and controlling.	You protect them by being obedient at the expense of independent thinking.	You are stubborn, resist cooperating, and tend to always have a contrary point of view.	You are bossy, demanding, and controlling toward others.
They were excessively critical of you.	You protect them by readily accepting blame for things that are not your fault. You become extremely cautious.	You deny that anything is ever your fault. For you, there is no constructive criticism.	You are quick to find fault with others, and rarely compliment anyone.

They reject you when you try to be close or dependent on them.	You protect them by becoming totally self-reliant and by avoiding help from others.	You insist on getting your demands met. You don't consider the needs of others.	You push people away when they want to depend on you.
They were weak, needy or incompetent.	You protect them by becoming overly responsible, taking charge, and by being unable to delegate responsibility	You rebelled by becoming insensitive to people, and don't listen to people's problems or complaints.	You present yourself as weak, always needing others to solve your problems.
Your parent vicariously lived through your accomplishments, and/or required that you be perfect.	You protect them from disappointment by showing off and being a know-it-all. You are driven to be perfect and can't tolerate mistakes in yourself and others.	You rebel by underperforming or failing.	You demand perfection of those with whom you work.
Your parent acts superior, and is contemptuous of others as a way of boosting his/her self-worth.	You protect them by acting silly and inappropriate, yelling, or acting out of control. The purpose is to allow your parent to feel superior to you.	You offend others by showing how morally virtuous you are.	You are quick to highlight the moral failings of those you work with.
Your parent or sibling is amoral.	You protect them by not following the rules and becoming dishonest.	You become excessively intolerant of anyone who doesn't follow the rules. This rigidity makes it difficult for others to work for you.	You use people and will do anything to get what you want.

column describes how failure can result from *mimicking* a parent who failed or did poorly in a business or profession, or never could effectively manage money.

You're familiar with the way *accommodating, rebelling, and mimicking* can promote other self-defeating behaviors such as overeating or difficulties establishing close relationships. Here you're seeing how the same things can undermine your success with your ambition, education, career, and creation of wealth.

Accommodation

Did you grow up in a family where your parent or sibling always bemoaned his or her bad luck with money, career, or business? You know, the one who's always making excuses or blaming others for his or her lack of success. "If only I had bought that stock, I'd be rich today." "If not for that S.O.B. who screwed me, I'd be head of the department" . . . or CEO, or have received a raise, or . . . you can probably fill in the blank yourself. Did you ever stop and think how it made you feel to have a parent or sibling who was unsuccessful with money and/or business? Do you think it's possible for this to *not* have a lasting effect on your life?

Being exposed to a parent or sibling who was bitter about his or her failings with money and success, and who was also threatened by your ambition, intelligence, and accomplishments, is bound to make you feel guilty enough to prevent you from achieving success and wealth for yourself. Or, if you do, you might have so much anxiety about it that you don't enjoy it or you sabotage what you've accomplished.

If you *accommodated* a parent or sibling who needed you to be perfect, you might easily have become a workaholic driven to perfection. If that's the case, you're likely to create resentment in those who work for you by unmercifully driving them and never being satisfied with their accomplishments.

Failing to succeed with money and career can also result from *rebelling* against the pressure to succeed at all costs by parents who live through your accomplishments. You might think that there are only advantages to being the "apple of their eye." Think again. If your parents became upset when you weren't perfect, or agitated if you made the slightest mistake in one of your sports games or hit a wrong note in a music recital, you know it wasn't so great to be so special to them.

"Dad, I got an A– on my exam; I really knew my stuff." "How come you didn't get an A? Next time study more." "I see you won your tennis match 6–2, 6–3; your backhand could have been stronger." Get the picture? What does that cause in job settings? You'll feel anxiety when you have a job interview, take a test, or perform in front of a group. The anxiety is a result of worrying that if you aren't perfect, you'll hurt your parents and cause them to feel like failures.

What do you do about it? You *rebel* against the pressure they put on you. You drop out, you fail, you become a druggie, you get into a counterculture lifestyle. Do they get the meaning of your protest? Hardly. After all, by failing, you're undermining their self-esteem, which we know depends on your achievements. Instead, in order to not feel disappointed by your rebellion, they respond by intensifying the pressure on you to succeed. And so the cycle of resentment and rebellion goes on and on.

What if your struggle for success (or money, and/or ambition) is a result of *mimicking*? You feel sorry for someone in your family who failed miserably with his or her career. It's just not fair that your life worked out and your relative's didn't. What makes matters worse is when you feel that somehow you contributed to the failure of the family member you feel sorry for. Your guilt about being better off than the other intensifies and causes you to undermine your achievements.

That's what happened to George—remember him from earlier in the book, the one who suffered from survivor guilt? George had a hard time enjoying his life because he felt so sorry for his brother who'd been born with a severe physical disability. After his brother died, George finally felt relief.

But let's go deeper and see how our past family situations cause our present career problems.

The Pain of Remembering: A Prosperous Tourist in the Midst of Poverty

Imagine you're a tourist visiting the sights in a poor country. You sit down to eat a delicious meal at an outdoor restaurant in the town square. As you're eating, a group of very poor, malnourished children and adults approaches to beg for money. You watch as flies cover their parched lips and flit around the children's swollen bellies. As you look from one sad, hungry face to another, a number of responses come into play for you, all reflecting your guilt over being better off. Maybe you lose your appetite. Maybe you feel compelled to give the people money. Maybe you leave as soon as possible. Though the actual situation is short-lived, you find yourself thinking about it a lot. It remains in your memory for a long time, and recalling it at a later date, you'll experience the awful feelings associated with it. That's why you'd rather forget it.

Rule to Remember: We try to forget the painful experiences of our childhood. What happens then is they remain hidden. What the above example illustrates is: One of the reasons people prevent themselves from succeeding in careers, financially, and/or socially is that they just feel too guilty about being better off than others.

How can you use this information to your advantage? By examining your past you now realize that you're particularly sensitive to anyone who's pathetic or jealous of you. This could be, for example, a lover, an employee, a co-worker. Once you recognize that some of your self-defeating reactions to people in your life are actually due to sensitivities that started in your family, you'll stop limiting yourself because you know your present-day responses don't fit your present-day situations.

You may not even be aware that your difficulty in advancing your career is related to negative personality qualities that you've developed. From dealing with superiors to dealing with customers, these qualities cut you off at the knees when it comes to your effectiveness in any area of your work life. The following list highlights twelve qualities and the way they can interfere with your goals.

Twelve Negative Personality Qualities That Can Undermine Your Success

You Don't Think Creatively or Independently   As a child you *accommodated* a domineering parent. As a result, you grew up to be afraid of asserting yourself, thinking for yourself, and acting independently. When you tried acting independently, you were afraid that you'd drive your fragile parent over the edge, causing him or her to scream and lose control. So you became submissive, you compromised your ability to think independently or be effective, and that is where you are today.

Today, whenever you start feeling uncomfortable about thinking independently, solving problems, or offering your opinions, you can overcome these limitations by applying what you have discovered about yourself.

You Are Inflexible and Demand Total Obedience and Submission from Others   Why does your department or company have low morale? On the surface, things seem to be under control because of your authoritarian ways. But a closer look reveals that the only people who work for you are those who are submissive or who aren't able to think independently or creatively. You're not able to delegate authority, and you have to be in charge. Workers won't bring problems to your attention if they assume the solutions conflict with your requirements. They know you're unlikely to consider ideas that don't agree with your own and that proposing ideas different from yours will probably provoke you.

You need to learn whether you've developed these qualities by *mimicking* a parent who was also authoritarian, *accommodating* a parent who was ineffectual, or *rebelling* against a parent who wanted you to be compliant.

You Have to Be Right   Always insisting you're right undermines your potential for success because it alienates people. Where does this trait have its origins? Did you become this way to please a parent who needed you to know everything and be perfect? Admitting mistakes would have disappointed your parent and made you feel guilty. Or does your need to be right have its roots as a rebellion against parents who were stupid and usually wrong? Of course, you might have mimicked a parent who was a know-it-all and always had to be right about everything.

You Are a Perfectionist   In excess, this quality makes it impossible to lead others. You'll drive yourself and others too hard, missing the forest for the trees as you try to keep track of every small detail. How did you get to be this way?

Your parents had such high standards that whatever you did wasn't quite good enough. Or they lived through your accomplishments: The more you achieved, the happier they were.

There it is, *if* you *accommodated* them. But how would *rebellion* account for your perfectionism? If your parents made fun of you when you made mistakes, or enjoyed your failures, or were very competitive with you, you would defy them by becoming perfect so that they couldn't enjoy your mistakes. Finally, you might have *mimicked* a parent with the same perfectionist qualities.

You Refuse to Accept Advice   You think of your antiauthoritarian attitude as the virtue of someone who is independent. Think again. Usually it's a justification for your defiant attitude. You may have developed this quality as a *rebellion* against an authoritarian parent. The result is that you experience every suggestion as an order to submit. Or, you may have developed this quality as an *accommodation* to a parent whose satisfaction resulted from your being smart and right. Then there's the possibility that you *mimicked* a parent who behaved this way by making the quality your own.

You Are Afraid to Speak Up When You Know the Answer   If you behave this way, it's hard for you to create a strong impression. Therefore, you undermine other people's impressions of you. Why do you do this? If your parents were overly critical, you might have feared humiliation when you ventured an opinion. You'd feel especially cautious about speaking up if your parent was competitive with you and couldn't stand for anyone else to be in the limelight. If you had a sibling or parent who was slow, or had a learning disability, you might feel guilty for showing how much you knew because you knew it would make them feel insecure. Or you may have *rebelled* against extreme expectations that you would be independent by instead going along with the consensus. If you had a parent who rarely spoke out, or rarely spoke up for him- or herself, you could be mimicking this quality out of sympathy and because you didn't want to outshine him or her.

Whenever you start to feel uncomfortable about speaking up, you now know that you can overcome this limitation by applying what you have discovered about yourself.

You Are a Chronic Liar   Imagine how this particular quality undermines your effectiveness. When people can't trust you, how successful can you ever be? How did you develop this quality? Perhaps you had a parent who always needed to look good and was vulnerable to having his or her flaws exposed. Wouldn't you learn to lie to protect that parent's false pride, thereby *accommodating* that parent's needs? Wouldn't you be also be inclined to lie to protect others around you from exposure to the truth?

What if your parent was critical of you? Instead of accepting blame, you rebelled by lying all the time to deflect the criticism. Through *rebellion,* you became a chronic liar. What if your parent rigidly required that you tell the truth no matter what the circumstances? You could have *rebelled* as a protest and become a chronic liar. But don't overlook the possibility that you might be *mimicking* a parent who was also a chronic liar.

You Are Exceedingly Mistrustful   How can you be effective managing others if you don't trust anyone? If your parent expects you to trust *only* him or her, you can *accommodate* by becoming exceedingly mistrustful of others. In that way you reassure your parent that you are loyal. But maybe your mistrust resulted from a *rebellion* against parents who were exceedingly trusting of others and were easily taken advantage of. You decided to mistrust others so you yourself would never be duped. Finally, you could be *mimicking* a mistrustful parent.

You Never Give Anyone Credit for His or Her Accomplishments This quality is bound to alienate people who work for you because it will thoroughly undermine morale. Really, why do a good job if it is not appreciated? Did this quality develop as a result of *mimicking* parents who are jealous of others' accomplishments? It could also have resulted from *accommodating* parents who are self-effacing and can't stand being admired. But, most often, the strongest motivation to avoid giving credit to others comes from *rebelling* against parents or siblings who are self-centered and always need to be admired.

You Complain All the Time Is this any way to promote yourself? You have to know that this behavior is *bound* to cause others to resent you, rather than respect you and look up to you. Where did it come from? It could have been an *accommodation* to a parent who needed to feel superior and in control, and who complained in order to feel superior. It could have been *rebellion* that developed as a protest against parents who demanded that you keep your problems to yourself. By complaining, you hoped they would get the message and become more sympathetic. Finally, you could be *mimicking* a parent who was a chronic whiner and complainer, or enjoyed talking about his or her physical symptoms.

You Like to Boast and Show Off No doubt about it, this quality will absolutely affect your ability to be liked and in a very negative way. This quality made a parent happy who was depressed and withdrawn, but who cheered up when you showed off. If your parent or sibling was inadequate, shy, or the like and vicariously enjoyed it when you were the center of attention, you'd have had an incentive to accommodate by showing off. If your parent preferred that you be shy and retiring, you might have resented it and *rebelled* by boasting.

Of course, you could also have *mimicked* a parent who was a show-off.

You Don't Listen to Others   It's extremely hard to lead if you can't stand listening to others. Whether you *mimicked* a parent who avoided listening to what others had to say, or you *rebelled* against listening to a parent or sibling who was needy, complaining, or dependent on you, you can now become more responsive to others. The knowledge you take away from assessing yourself should help you to overcome your assumption that everyone else in your life will become excessively dependent on you. When you change your attitude, you'll find others will see you as a caring person.

Now it's time to go back and study the previous chart in order to see which mechanisms are undermining your success. Seeing the truth will help make it easier for you to fulfill your potential to become successful.

Can You Compete Successfully?

Competition exists in every relationship we have in the world. We even compete with the rest of creation for our place on earth. How well we compete determines whether we will live, reproduce, and create future generations to carry on after we're gone.

Competition in families is a natural offshoot of this truth. Dominance and submission, rivalry and cooperation, opposition and participation are all aspects of competition within the family. Our position in our family and our sense of self-worth are caught up in this issue. But since we develop an understanding of these things when we are quite young, we need an internal system of assessment to help us know where we stand vis-à-vis our competition.

In order to move ahead at full speed, you have to be able

to assess whether your success is making the other person involved feel weak, jealous, or threatened. But just as in other parts of our lives, guilt can surface in competition, too, and hold us back. What belief is contributing this time? The belief that someone has been hurt and it's your fault. How we oppose someone and the way we go about winning (or losing) is pretty much determined by our guilt, or the lack of it, around competing.

Just wanting to defeat an opponent doesn't necessarily make us feel guilty enough to stop ourselves from competing or to make us compete ineffectively. We don't always have to hold back our successes or diminish our abilities. Sometimes we can also prevent ourselves from feeling happy when we do something well. If our opponent is truly weak, competition will seem unfair. A poor loser may try to take advantage of this by communicating that he or she is weak, hurt, and diminished by the experience of losing. This causes us to feel guilty and spoils our sense of accomplishment.

Contrast this with someone who, in losing graciously, makes it possible for you to enjoy your victory without feeling guilty. Obviously, he or she enjoyed the competition and didn't feel wounded as a result of losing. When a competitor is confident and strong, you're less likely to feel guilty, and therefore it'll be easier for you to win and, when you do, enjoy the experience.

Just as we can usually gauge the strength of our competitors as adults, as children we are also able to correctly perceive the strengths and weaknesses of our parents and siblings. It's something that we know unconsciously—parents who are confident and happy make it possible for their children to pursue their personal goals more fully. Seeing a loved one hurt by our normal behavior and goals usually causes us to put the brakes on our abilities, even at the expense of our best interests.

This dynamic is clear when a couple divorces. Where do the children thrive? With the parent who makes the best adjustment. Where do they have the most trouble? With the parent whose suffering worries them or makes them feel sorry for him or her. And even though the other parent may be preferred, often the child will feel obligated to take the side of the wounded parent from fear that that parent will feel *even more* damaged if the other parent is favored.

If you're a parent with a child of the same sex, watch your child compete with you for the affection of your spouse. If you're a male and your son, age four to seven, says he wants you to go away so he can marry Mommy, you can think of it as either charming or threatening. The first response will help your child to feel confident about competing with you because he perceives your strength. The second response may have a disturbing effect on him because he'll worry about hurting you. Your reaction causes your son to perceive you as either strong or weak.

As an example of past pain, let's look at the case of Rick, who felt that his childhood successes ruined life for his brother.

■ RICK ■

Rick was undermining his own achievements. Rick's father was always critical of Rick's brother, Paul—excessively so. Paul was unsuccessful in school and often in trouble with the authorities. Rick believed Paul's suffering was worse whenever Paul was compared to Rick. As an adult, Rick blocked out those memories because they made him feel guilt about his sibling (an example of present pain). What was the result? Rick was unable to change his pattern of undermining his successes (an example of future pain). Pain—past, present and future—kept Rick from recognizing how he was defeating himself.

But Rick wasn't responsible for his brother's difficulties, so why would he blame himself for Paul's problems when he wasn't at fault? It was all done in the hope of relieving his brother's suffering and his father's distress with Paul. Limiting his achievements was Rick's way of doing this.

If, like Rick, you believed that being smart in school was threatening to your brother, then getting good grades would make you feel guilty. You'd feel you were showing your brother up and therefore causing him pain. The result would be that you would hold yourself back from getting those good grades you were capable of getting. This behavior would be reinforced if your brother acted hurt by your success or was overtly envious of you.

What if you felt pressured by your father to restrain your success so you brother would feel better about himself? Then your thinking might be, "I'd better not excel so my father won't feel so bad about my brother." Or you could hold yourself back to protect your father from feeling shame over his failing son. In this case, your new rule would be "Success is a negative" or "Modesty is a positive." This code would restrict your behavior now, as it did then.

But what a huge price you would pay! In response to this new rule, you'd hate yourself for doing poorly in school and feel like a sinner if you did well. You'd experience this dilemma even though you weren't really responsible for your brother's difficulties.

But there's another way you could solve this problem. You could atone for your sin of success in school, athletics, or social life by trying to rescue your brother (and any other brother figure that you come across in your life).

You might take time out of your life to tutor your brother, even if it meant depriving yourself of enough study time. Continuing the behavior as an adult, you might become known as Mr. or Ms. Rescue. But if in the process of rescuing others you sacrificed too much of your time or yourself, you'd end up feeling resentful. And then, naturally, you'd hate yourself for feeling this way. Guilt would make it hard for you to *not* meet the requests of others, even if they were unreasonable. And salespeople, people needing money, or just about anyone needing help would be impossible for you to refuse.

Why does the past behavior of our family members continue to affect us even when we aren't exposed to their negative reinforcement? Why do we keep up our negative patterns even as adults, living away from our parents and siblings, or even long after our parents have died? Why are our guilt feelings so hard to overcome? Another look at Rick may help shed some light on the problem of why we allow behavior that we truly hate to continue into our adult life.

My first meeting with Rick didn't reveal the depth of his problem, but as we talked I began to see what had caused his difficulties. In spite of Rick's being intelligent and well educated, his declaration of being a "failure" caused me to ask a simple question, "How are you failing?" Rick said, "I've set up my office several times, and each time it's gone bust." He added, "I feel plagued by an inability to be successful. I've had great training. I know my stuff. But when it comes to putting everything together, somehow I always blow it." When I asked, "Have you always had trouble succeeding? Did you have difficulty in school, as a boy?" "No," he answered, "Just the opposite. My brother had problems in that area, but I always did really well in school. In fact, I was sort of this 'star' of our family that way. You know, good athlete, strong learner, popular." Probing, I said, "Tell me about your brother." Half sighing and with a shake of his head, Rick said, "Paul always got into trouble. He misbehaved in school, even when he was really young. As a result, he always brought home terrible report cards. Dad would become enraged and eventually would beat Paul."

Rick confessed that he "hated" that, saying, "I always felt sorry for Paul. Dad would hit him and yell, 'Why can't you be like your brother? Why do you always screw up?' I wished Paul could do better, too. But more, I wished Dad would leave me out of it. It made me sick to my stomach to hear Dad yelling that way."

Rick's original thought, "My success hurts my brother," grew into a general idea, "It is wrong to outdo anyone." That idea in turn evolved into the mind-set "Ambition is bad." Rick *then* found a way of hiding from this negative emotion (and the pain of his childhood) by transforming it into a more socially acceptable value such as "Always help others." And while "Always help others" may be morally admirable, it can also be self-destructive if you routinely sacrifice your own interests for others.

You may not even know that you're burdened with a mind-set about not being successful. The only thing you *are* conscious of is that you're frustrated at your inability to succeed. But remember, being consciously aware of the moral value "Success is wrong" might remind you of having hurt your sibling. And because this memory is painful, you keep putting it out of your mind.

"Success is wrong" was the value beneath the surface of Rick's consciousness, and, sadly, because he linked his own success with damaging his brother's life, Rick damaged his own too. Equally sad was the fact that Rick's failing did *not* protect his brother. Paul's difficulties continued into adulthood, and his lack of achievement became the limiting factor for both brothers. Had Paul become successful in his adult life, Rick would have felt relieved and less burdened by his feelings of guilt towards Paul.

But the power of Rick's mind-set was strong, and it resulted in the following series of failures, despite his best efforts: When choosing a site for his first office, he located, against advice not to, in an area where there were too many other practitioners for the population. Then, after relocating to a second office, he hired too large a staff, and his practice sank under his unusually high overhead. In his third try, Rick employed people with too little experience, and then, even though he knew he had to, Rick found himself unable to fire those who were either incompetent or difficult to get along with.

Maybe you're thinking, these are just examples of inexperience, not really the inability to succeed. But remember, Rick came to me because he knew he *wasn't able* to succeed. In his case, positive reinforcement became the real stumbling block to Rick's success. It started back with his father. Pleasing him meant making things bad for Paul. On the other hand, trying to save his brother pain and humiliation meant disappointing his father: a no-win situation and another example of *double trouble*.

Would positive advice from a standard self-help book have been helpful to Rick? Would testimonials or exercises in positive reinforcement have enabled him to overcome his destructive mind-set? No. Positive reinforcement was Rick's Achilles heel, and no amount of hand-clapping and back-patting praise would ever have helped him. Nothing helped until Rick uncovered the hidden truths of his family history and how they played themselves out in his adult life. ▪

What about people you know who *can* attain success but *can't* hold onto it once they've got it? Why does this happen to them? Or perhaps it happens to you. Reading on and understanding William's story may help you make sense of this.

▦ WILLIAM ▦

William was reacting to other people's envy. Smart, talented, highly educated, and a partner in a law firm, William eroded his good will with the other partners. The result was that he began to see referrals diminishing in his specialized practice. He also noticed that in the past three years, the high regard he had been held in by his clients had likewise diminished. William truly had no idea what accounted for this shift in his fortunes. Instead, he kept reminding himself of his special skills, unique education, and network of referral sources. These reminders helped him reassure himself and ward off the anxiety he was feeling about losing his influence and income.

William was referred to me by his family physician after his wife complained to him that William was becoming increasingly depressed and that she was concerned about his future at his firm. At the first visit, I asked William if he could be more specific about what he was struggling with. He said that over the past year he had become increasingly unhappy. During that time, some of the partners criticized him for his lack of participation and communication, and that started William's worrying and pessimism about his status at the firm. "How long has this been going on?" I asked. He said for about three years— but he couldn't identify any particular cause.

It soon became evident that William had grown up in a very troubled family, yet like a fly that freed itself from a spider's web, he had escaped from its damaging influence. Surprisingly, William was unaware that he had been adversely affected by three major life events: first by the death of his mother *three years earlier,* then by his father's death four months later, and finally by his next older brother's death three months after that.

Asked which of the deaths had the biggest impact on him, William said it was his dad's death. He wished he could have had a better relationship with him. "He kept trying to do well but could never succeed." With that comment, I wondered (and probably at this point in the book, you are wondering too) if his relationship with his father had contributed to his problems at work.

Here are the facts William gave me about his father. At one time he had been a moderately successful businessman, but that was before becoming a chronic alcoholic. This became the major cause of his failure in his career and his difficulties in the family. He went into drunken rages at night, where he would typically scream at and demean every one of his five sons. William's father never formed close relationships with anyone and found fault with everyone but himself. He was very insecure, lacked a sense of his own worth, and openly envied anyone who was more successful than he was. Putting other people down helped him feel more important and helped him deny that he was envious of those who were more successful than he.

And William? The more he achieved in school and later in his career, the more his father found fault with him. The result? William couldn't get close to his father because he felt he could never please him or do things right. William did not *consciously* realize that his father was envious of him, even though his father had always acted this way.

William's father died a failure, leaving William with lifelong guilt for outdoing him professionally, financially, and personally. After his father's death, William felt even worse because now he had no way of ever reconciling with him. But this was only one of the factors that set William up for the pattern of his recent self-destructive behavior. There was also his next older brother, Matt.

As long as William could remember, Matt was a rebel. He was the one who always broke the rules. At home, Matt challenged their dad, which provoked his alcoholic rages. In high school Matt used and dealt drugs. He committed burglaries, and several times he spent time in jail. Eventually, Matt died of a drug overdose.

As a child, Matt had always been competitive with William, but always came in second best. Matt didn't lack intelligence, either. In fact, he was really bright, as well as being charming and charismatic. But his stubborn and headstrong ways required him to butt up against authority, and this was the source of all his problems as well as his downfall.

Of William's three younger brothers, one had died twenty years earlier from alcoholism, another was severely mentally ill, and the last dropped out of high school and was doing mechanical work for a company. Amazingly, William seemed to have emerged unscathed from this emotional quicksand. He had become highly educated and a good father and responsible husband. Just as amazingly, William seemed to have escaped the effects of survivor guilt—the guilt that we saw makes people feel that it's unfair for them to have succeeded when everyone close to them succumbed to tragedy.

Sometimes a family death (or deaths) can have an *immediate* negative effect on a person's life, causing depression or agitation. This wasn't the way it was for William. His father's death only gradually intensified William's ongoing sensitivity to something he'd

experienced all his life from his father and his brother—
envy. And so they died, taking their envy of William to
their graves and leaving William with big issues
unresolved. But since their lifelong envy of him didn't
prevent William from achieving a lot in his life, I
wondered what other factors were influencing William's
downward slide from success. That's when I heard about
Henry, William's partner and a lot more.

William and Henry had been friends and partners for
quite some time, and for a big part of that time, William
hadn't realized that Henry had been envious of him.
William's higher billings and bonuses were the cause of
that envy. When Henry decided to finally leave the firm to
join a company that their firm consulted with, William
said to me, "I think Henry was jealous of my success and
even resented my suggestions to him on how to increase
his business and billings."

Henry's effect on William had been profound, and he
said, "I assumed Henry left because of his jealousy of me
and because he thought I wasn't doing enough to help
him. I think he thought that I was contemptuous of him
and that he couldn't control me. Once Henry left, he acted
as if I had hurt him, and he ignored me." One time when
he bumped into Henry with one of the new firm's partners,
he said, "Henry tried to avoid me, like he felt guilty for
ignoring me. I thought he was embarrassed about seeing
me because he had left."

According to William, Henry's new job was much
more secure than the one he left, but the trade-off was that
he was paid much less. He would never make as much
money as William did. When I asked William how he felt
about that, he said being so much better off made him
uncomfortable.

What did William do to fix his "uncomfortable" (read

"guilty") feeling? He began spoiling his relationships within the firm and with his clients. Doing less well financially, William would *accommodate* Henry by putting himself in the same financial situation that Henry was in. Henry was also the substitute for William's brother and father, both of whom had envied William's success. William began to understand why he was so upset over Henry's exit from the firm. He had been so sensitized by a lifetime of envy from his father and brother that he wasn't able to appreciate that his experience with Henry still could possibly have such a profound effect on him. Yet it did.

Once William understood why he was so troubled by his relationship with Henry, he quickly saw why he had undermined himself with his firm and his clients. He began to consciously apply this knowledge to reversing the destructive course he'd been on. Within one year he left his firm and joined another, where he established outstanding relationships with his clients and new partners and where he continues to thrive today.

Problems with money and success could start in the same place—the family—but end up in a dramatically different one. This was the case with Irene.

IRENE

Irene was destroying her sense of well-being. When it came to money, Irene was a wreck. Not only was she tight with money, but the more she had, the more nervous about it she became. Whereas most people find security in having money, Irene found only anxiety.

A successful lawyer who achieved a fair amount of financial success, Irene had a great deal of difficulty spending money on herself. Her exaggerated fear of losing money made it easier for her to save it than to spend it, which doesn't come as any surprise. The surprise came when Irene found herself growing more uneasy as her wealth *increased,* coupled with the fact that as her wealth increased, so did her overeating.

Irene was the only child of parents who were restaurant owners. During her childhood their business failed several times, creating an unstable and chaotic financial life for the family. Her parents were usually in debt, or working furiously to eliminate it. When they were out of debt, there was a constant worry about whether they'd make enough money for the future. Irene's father went through altenating periods of optimism and pessimism because his business income varied so enormously, and yet he never became severely distraught. That part was left for Irene's mother to play.

Irene's mother was often critical of her husband, blaming him constantly for their precarious financial situation and disparaging him for not doing as well as many of their friends and relatives. She was quite open in her envy of people with money, acted victimized by her circumstances, and smoked and binged with food whenever her worries overcame her. Though she was responsible for most of the business decisions, including locations, menu, and staff, she blamed her husband when things didn't work out.

Irene recognized that her mother's suffering affected her, Irene, the most. It wasn't that their relationship was in conflict; rather, her mother's constant anxiety distracted her from a better emotional connection with her daughter. Because Irene's father didn't receive support and understanding from his wife, he became distant from her and established a better emotional connection with his daughter, who was sympathetic, friendly, playful, and calm.

Unconsciously, Irene felt uncomfortable that her relationship with her father seemed closer than the one her mother had with him. She worried that this would add to her mother's unhappiness, and she didn't want to think that she was in any way a cause for further tension between her parents. Of course, she couldn't know that the tensions between her parents were totally independent of her.

Irene worried about her mother. She tried comforting her by offering suggestions about how to make the restaurant more successful, and tried consoling her by reassuring her that things would work out in the future. The problem was, her mother, a chronic complainer, was not easily placated. Even when business conditions *did* improve, she worried constantly about how things might go wrong.

Starting at a young age, Irene worked part-time in the restaurant during the school year, as well as during the summer when she was in high school. Because of her mother's angst, Irene began to overvalue the importance of every dollar that she earned and saved. She was determined never to be vulnerable to financial insecurity the way her mother had been. The result? Irene became driven and controlled by money. Her sole concerns were about making it and losing it. All her ambitions to succeed were reinforced by her parents, who strongly pushed for her to become a professional so that she would be immune to the financial problems and lack of status that they (her mother in particular) had endured.

Irene did very well in law school, was hired by a prominent law firm, and after several years became a partner. A workaholic, Irene was attentive to her clients, respected by her partners, and increasingly successful in her firm.

Why, then, did she come to see me? Irene really wanted to overcome her anxiety, occasional depressed moods, and bouts of overeating. Though she was smart and analytical, Irene wasn't able to make the specific connections between her anxiety, her overeating, and her mother's angst and suffering over the family's financial uncertainty. Once she saw the parallel, Irene began recognizing the irony of their different circumstances. "Why do I worry so much when I'm secure in my career?"

Do you see it? Remember that her mother's unhappiness made Irene feel uncomfortable. This was because it made her feel guilty about being so much better off than her mother. So, if she assumed the same worries about losing her wealth, and if she, too, binged with food when counting her money, it would be a way of placing herself in the same situation as her anxious mother. By mimicking her mother she wouldn't have to experience guilt feelings about being better off than her mother or worry that she was envied.

What about the great irony of Irene? The greater her wealth, the greater her insecurity. What was that about? Her sense of guilt about being well off required her to think that she would lose her wealth, instead of feeling more financially secure. Remember, her parents could never feel financially secure because of the precarious nature of their business. The good financial years were always followed by years of failure. As Irene began understanding these dynamics, her anxiety decreased and she developed a greater sense of well-being.

Irene *mimicked* her mother's suffering as a way of undoing her guilt about feeling better off than her long-suffering mother. Unlike others who undermine their success as an *accommodation* to guilt, Irene achieved her goals of financial success, only to spoil the sense of well-being that accompanied it. ■

We move on to Jack, who was a rebel as a child and was still rebelling as an adult, but with greater consequences to his career and his family.

■ JACK ■

Jack was stuck in his risk-taking life. Jack was a married engineer who voluntarily sought help from his doctor for cocaine use. It was causing weight loss, headaches, ringing in his ears, and irritability; it was also undermining his career. His doctor told me that he thought Jack didn't seem severely enough addicted to require a residential treatment program at this time. It was his opinion that Jack's continued use was not really motivated by physical addiction but instead by psychological factors.

When Jack came to see me, he told me he was very concerned that his drug use might be affecting his work and possibly his marriage. He was less worried about the weight loss and physical symptoms, and he also had his doubts about how serious his addiction really was because he could voluntarily stop using cocaine for a month at a time. That said, Jack would inevitably be lured back to using coke again and again, but *not* because he felt withdrawal symptoms.

Sometimes Jack's motivation was recreational, and sometimes it was to get release from job stress. But Jack also explained that he enjoyed cocaine because it made him feel that he was free from the rules that everyone else had to follow. When I asked him to say more, Jack simply replied, "I like to be the rebel, to take risks." Jack even told me that when he felt the drug was beginning to control him, he'd become angry and resentful.

Jack was determined not to let anything, *including a drug,* control him.

One of Jack's major issues was his need to rebel against being controlled either by a person or a drug. *Rebellion* against convention caused him to be attracted to the drug, helping him "feel free of the rules that everyone else had to follow." Jack said, "In the past, when I rebelled, there weren't the serious consequences like with drug use." Resentment against being controlled also helped Jack *free* himself of cocaine's power over him. After he was off the drug for a while, he'd begin thinking that he was staying clean just because it was expected of him. So to counter the feeling he had that he was pleasing others, he'd rebel and return to using. What were the reasons for his need to be a rebel and to sometimes take unnecessary risk to acquire the drug?

Jack had difficulties in his work and his marriage, but he didn't see that these problems and his drug use had similar origins. Discussing his career, Jack said he worried that he was lazy, because he'd become bored after working on a project for a while. As a result, Jack felt that he was wasting his skills and ruining his reputation. "What do you mean by lazy?" I asked. He said that his attitude would alternate between diligent attention to the needs of his clients and loss of interest in the project he was working on. What did he think accounted for the shift to boredom, and what was it that diminished his involvement after feeling so enthusiastic at the beginning of a project?

It's true that at first Jack *did* feel enthusiastic, but he'd also worry that he wasn't doing enough to please his client. In response, Jack would work harder and harder until he finally started to resent the client because he felt he was putting out too much effort. This caused him to *rebel* by paying less attention to the work. But he also felt guilty about paying less attention to his job, and that's what made him think he was lazy. Sometimes the same mechanism of pleasing and rebelling against pleasing would become more intense when he felt caught between the competing requirements of the client, the planning bureaucrats, and the contractor. Clearly, Jack was burdened by his excessive sense of responsibility, to which he responded with rebellious nonconformity.

In his family, Jack was the oldest of three children, and his mother looked to him to solve many of his siblings' problems. He felt obligated to meet her demands because his mother adored him. At the same time, Jack said, he felt burdened and resentful about having to meet his mother's expectations.

It was very hard for Jack to get recognition from his father when he did something well in school or sports. "I was always trying to please him, to earn his approval. Yet, to my mother, I was the perfect son. I could do no wrong. My mother adored me." "What do you think was the reason for your dad's attitude toward you?" I asked. Jack replied that he thought that his father resented him because of the attention paid to him by his mother.

Jack added, "I notice that when I do things that are good I denigrate them, and when people give me compliments I don't believe them. One reason for this was that the more his clients appreciated his work, the greater was his concern that they would expect more from him, leading to a greater likelihood that he would disappoint them.

I suggested that another reason for his not wanting to accept compliments from them was that in the past, when his mother admired him, he felt guilty for threatening his father's position in the family. Therefore he equated admiration from anyone with the admiration he received from his mother.

Why else did Jack undermine himself with cocaine? This problem was related to his younger brother. He'd gotten into serious trouble and had been sentenced to a lengthy prison term. Jack said, "My brother's life was a tragedy, but I survived. It has been very painful for me to see what he did to himself, and his family. I have tried to be a good uncle to his kids. I feel badly that I don't write to him more often." Was Jack suffering from survivor guilt because his brother had been self-destructive and destroyed his life but Jack hadn't and instead had thrived? Survivor guilt made it difficult for Jack to be happy and to do well, and the way he undermined himself was to take great risks to acquire the drug. Putting himself at risk of getting mugged, knifed, arrested, along with the prospect of losing his professional license, would be a way for Jack to ruin his life and relieve his guilt about being better off in his life than his brother. That was Jack's motivation for *mimicking* his brother. Once he saw that, Jack was able to address his self-defeating behaviors, put an end to them, and live his life more happily.

In this chapter you've read many stories of success and wealth and sometimes the lack of both. Where do you fit into the career, money, and success picture? Are you where you want to be in your career? Are you realizing your potential? Are you able to make the money you want, save what you want, invest what you want? If you are, congratulations: This is an area where you don't need to delve further. But if you're not answering yes to the questions just posed, let's see if we can start a process where saying yes becomes a not-so-distant possibility.

Exercise: Now Look at Yourself

What does success mean to you? What does it look like? Imagine now that you have it—but wait, there's a little problem imagining "it" when you don't have a clear picture of what "it" is.

Part 1

Let's define "it." You are now the editor of a new dictionary. And it's not Mr. Webster's or Ms. Collier's, it's the Dictionary of You. Your first word to define in this nonalphabetical dictionary is "success." Your entry for this word is personal, perhaps encompassing what you dream of, mixed with some of what you have, and/or maybe some of what you had but no longer *do* have.

Part 2

When you get to the end of your definition, add "see _____ ." To fill in the blank in order to further elaborate on your definition of "success," come up with a list. For example, "see: house in Hawaii, a horse stable, an art studio, a recording contract, an autographed Jackie Robinson baseball card, . . ."

Moving Ahead

If you've ever wondered why your children act in ways that they know will bring a negative response from you instead of doing what will make you happy, reading Chapter 16 will help you understand the "why" behind the behavior.

I've Become
My Mother/Father and
My Child Is a Pain

Do Any of These Parental Complaints Sound Familiar?

1. She refuses to listen to anything I say and I don't know what to do.
2. He's a whiner and I can't stand it.
3. He's such a wimp and a brownnoser; it disgusts me.
4. How can a girl who has such good looks be such a slob?
5. I don't understand why he's so aloof; he keeps all his feelings to himself.
6. Why is she such a know-it-all? No matter what I say, she always puts it down.
7. Every time our relationship is going well, she starts a fight. I can't believe that she always provokes me.

Why Do They Provoke instead of Please?

Though they seem to be very different, all of the complaints you've just read have one thing in common: the exasperation that many parents experience over behaviors in their kids that they can't stand but seem helpless to change. As a parent you've probably spent an enormous amount of time and also energy trying to figure out just why your children act in precisely the ways they know are guaranteed to bring on a full-blown negative response from you. It's probably caused you to spend time wondering why, when they know what will make you happy, *don't they just do it?*

Once you know which motivations are responsible for those of your kids' actions that you hate, and how they developed, you will have a better understanding and more control over your struggles with your kids. The charts that follow (starting on page 234) make it easy for you to grasp which aspects of your relationship with your children are the source of the behaviors that you can't stand.

By now you're very familiar with how accommodation, rebellion, and mimicking influence our behavior. Seeing how your own flaws (which are responses to problems in your original family) have affected your children shouldn't be so difficult.

It's Never Your Fault, Is It?

Isn't it supposed to be someone else's kids with all the serious problems? You're probably quick to criticize your neighbor or sister-in-law when one of their children behaves badly, does poorly in school, uses drugs, acts defiantly, is withdrawn, and so on. Your children couldn't possibly have these problems because, in contrast with the parents of those kids, you and your spouse are loving, conscientious, and encouraging. Summing it up, you two are great parents. Right? All of which works fine for you until *your* child starts to act badly; *your* child exasperates, provokes and enrages you; *your* child makes you feel disappointed, bitter, or lost. How do you respond? Do you blame your child? Do you blame fate? genetics? the devil? Do you suffer, act victimized, or blame your spouse? Or do you just ignore it?

Does the thought ever fly by that maybe, just maybe, it might be one of your *own* behaviors that is responsible for the problem? Most likely it's too painful to think that the cause of what you can't stand in your kids is *you*. What if you have been making them feel guilty about pursuing their normal activities or healthy behavior (inadvertently, of course)? What if you're causing them to rebel against you because of resentment about the way you're acting with them? Or what if you just couldn't resist mimicking the behaviors that you hated in your parents or siblings, and now you own kids are copying your self-defeating patterns? The problems are there, but so are the solutions; they're just hard to access because they involve getting in touch with memories and feelings from your childhood that are unpleasant and so have been buried deep inside.

Step Inside Yourself and Bring Your Flashlight

If you're provoked by your kid's behavior, you can either deny that it has anything to do with you, or you can look within yourself for the origins of the problem. Remember, just as you *accommodated, rebelled,* and *mimicked* the worst flaws of your parents and siblings, your children will do the same in response to *your* mistakes. The agitation you feel with your kids can be an important signal for you to examine your own life. If their confrontational behaviors go unchanged despite your punishments and rewards, you need to consider the way you have been parenting them.

Remember, they are experiencing unpleasant or painful interactions with you and they're communicating that to you through behavior, not words. Once you examine your faults in parenting, you can change them, and with that you can prevent your children's negative patterns from becoming permanently set.

Failings? What Failings? Clues to Your Failings as a Parent

You can often become aware of mistakes that you are likely to make with your kids by observing the following clues.

Have You Ever Had Pets?   If so, most likely you've seen yourself behaving toward them in ways that you disliked but couldn't change. Did you yell at them? Beat them? Were you too possessive of their affection and devotion, or cold and rejecting with them? When it came to feeding them, did you overdo it, or did you underfeed them? Were your reactions to their bodily functions too extreme? Did you go nuts over obedience training, or just ignore it, only to find yourself controlled by your pet later on? Were any of these patterns excessive? What situations provoked them?

If you answered yes to any of the above questions, you're looking at a rather large clue as to how you are, or will be, in your behavior toward your children. Why is this so important? Most parents are blind to their shortcomings with their kids, and therefore they're so surprised and so frustrated when their kids react to them with behaviors that they don't like and just can't explain.

Are You Too Easily Angered by the Specific Actions, Qualities, or Sayings of Others?   Whatever inflames you the most is usually the quality that you can't stand in yourself.

Do Your Kids Behave in Ways That Remind You of Yourself?   When your kids make you furious or disgusted, ask yourself if the behavior they are exhibiting is the same one that you can't stand in yourself. If your child is too much of an "apple polisher" and goes out of his or her way to please everyone, are you looking at one of the qualities you don't like in yourself? As you've already realized from reading this book, once you're in touch with your hidden flaws, you can begin to understand what's going wrong with your kids.

The rest of this chapter will help you identify the ways your shortcomings create the behaviors in your children that you can't tolerate. In the chart "When You Can't Stand Your Kids," the first column is the behaviors that provoke you, followed by explanations based on accommodating you, rebelling against you, and mimicking you.

Let's look at the first example: Your child is continually overeating and is significantly overweight. This could occur if a parent or sibling seems jealous of anyone who is more attractive than he or she is. So the child, not wanting to cause hurt, would become fat and/or stay fat. The second reason would be to please a parent who needs for his or her child to eat heartily because it's a sign of good parenting. So even the child who feels full won't stop eating so as not to disappoint the parent. Finally, a child might be fat because he or she feels sorry for (or guilty about) being more in control than the parent or sibling who is fat and miserable because of it. Which one applies to you?

When You Can't Stand Your Kids: Part Two

In the next chart, "Why Are My Kids a Continual Pain?" we're looking at the same question but with a different spin. This chart's first column is about what *you are doing to them*. In the columns that follow, you can see how your specific behavior is negatively affecting your children.

The second column describes how your children may *rebel* against you. For example, if you're a perfectionist, they'll rebel against the requirement to be perfect at all costs to themselves. Therefore, you'll notice behavior such as excessive sloppiness, making poor grades, and refusing to compete.

WHEN YOU CAN'T STAND YOUR KIDS

The Behavior that You Hate in Your Kids	When It Results from Excessively Pleasing You or a Sibling	When It Results from Rebelling and Protesting Against What You Expect	When It Results from Mimicking Your Flaw
They are fat and can't lose weight.	1. You or a sibling are self-centered about your appearance and jealous of people who are attractive. 2. You feel worthwhile when your child eats.	1. You are obsessed about their eating habits and need for them to be thin. 2. You withhold food or desserts as punishment.	You are fat and suffer because of it. Your child feels sorry for you, and may feel that he or she contributed to it
They are shy, insecure, and inadequate.	You or a sibling needs to brag and show off in order to feel worthwhile.	You need for them to be strong and the center of attention. They rebel by acting shy and insecure.	You are insecure and they feel sorry for you.
They show off and have to be the center of attention.	You live through their accomplishments.	You prefer that they be seen and not heard, stay in the background. They rebel by showing off.	You are a big show off and need to be the center of attention.
They whine and complain.	You need to feel superior. They give you reason to be contemptuous of them.	You are unresponsive to their needs because you feel burdened by them.	You or a sibling act like the victim, suffer and complain continuously.

234

They are too obedient and give in too easily. They don't think for themselves.	You are too authoritarian, controlling, bossy, and rigid.	You expect them to be noncon-formists. They rebel with compliant behavior.	You are a "yes man" and do whatever is expected of you.
They are too controlling and bossy.	You are ineffectual and out of control. They take over and run the show.	You expect them to be compliant, to compromise, and to give in.	You are too rigid and controlling.
They are stubborn, defiant, and refuse to give in or compromise.	You expect them to be independent and not be influenced by others.	You are too controlling and authoritarian.	You are stubborn and defiant.
They are aloof and avoid intimacy with others.	1. You are rejecting and cold. 2. You compete with your child for the attention of your spouse.	You are too possessive, and want them to be closer to you than to anyone else.	You are aloof and avoid intimacy with others.
They are needy and dependent.	You baby them and are uncomfortable with their independence from you.	You are rejecting and cold, and want them to stay emotionally distant from you.	You are a dependent and needy person.
They steal or cheat.	You act morally superior to others.	You used or deprived them. They rebelled by stealing or cheating to get what they wanted.	You are dishonest, and cheat and steal.
They are mistrustful of others.	You expect them to trust and depend mainly on you.	You are overly naïve, trusting, and easily taken advantage of.	You are mistrustful and paranoid.

WHEN YOU CAN'T STAND YOUR KIDS (continued)

The Behavior that You Hate in Your Kids	When It Results from Excessively Pleasing You or a Sibling	When It Results from Rebelling and Protesting Against What You Expect	When It Results from Mimicking Your Flaw
They select friends who tend to reject them.	You are jealous and hurt if they prefer others to you.	You live through them and expect them to have perfect relationships.	You were rejected and hurt by your spouse. You or your spouse may have rejected a sibling.
They avoid showing their feelings.	You are insensitive to their feelings and/or reject them.	You or a sibling is depressed and needy of sympathy and care. They rebel by not showing their feelings.	You are indifferent to others' pain or complaints.
They rescue and feel overly compassionate toward people and animals.	You are needy, unhappy, or mistreated, and need attention.	You are indifferent to the suffering of others.	You are a "do gooder" and rescuer.
They are never satisfied with their achievements and need to be perfect.	You live through their accomplishments, and expect perfection.	You make fun of their mistakes. You can't stand anyone else's success.	You have to be perfect, and you drive yourself unmercifully.

They are extremely vigilant, and can't stand emotional instability or intoxication.	You are emotionally unpredictable, and may be a drug or alcohol abuser.	You are in denial about danger, or whenever a crisis occurs you don't respond appropriately.	You are continually anxious, vigilant, worried, or paranoid.
They lie consistently.	You are vulnerable and embarrassed about the exposure of your flaws. You need to always look good to the world.	1. You are too rigid or insistent about telling the truth no matter what the cost. 2. You are quick to point out their flaws, or make fun of them.	You are a liar and rarely tell the truth.

WHY ARE MY KIDS A CONTINUAL PAIN? (continued)

What You Do to Them	When They Rebel	When They Accommodate	When They Mimic
You are too critical.	They refuse to listen to you and deny your accusations.	They accept your accusations: "I'm selfish, no good, lazy, rotten, dishonest, etc."	They are critical of you.
You demand perfection and live through their accomplishments.	They are sloppy, do poorly on tests or sports, and are careless. They may become fat.	They are driven to succeed at everything, but always anxious because they fear disappointing you if they fall short.	They expect perfection from you. In their eyes, you always fall short.
You are cold and rejecting.	They demand attention at all costs no matter how destructively they have to act to achieve it.	They become excessively independent, and distant from people. They are cold and disapproving.	They reject you.
You act possessive toward them.	They stay away from you and keep emotionally distant from you. They prefer and admire others.	They are loyal to you, cling to you, and have difficulty leaving home. (This can also manifest in a school phobia.)	They act possessive toward you, don't want you to show an interest in others.
You are needy and depressed.	They become indifferent to complaints or suffering.	They become overly attentive to you and go overboard to make you happy.	They are needy, whiny, or complain unless you show concern.

You are self-centered, always focusing on yourself and your own importance.	They never give you credit for your accomplishments.	They avoid taking credit, remain in the background, and show excessive admiration for you.	They must always be the most important in the group and expect adulation.
You are shy to a fault.	They take center stage.	They try to bring you out.	They are shy and unassuming.
You are submissive and usually give in to their requests.	They don't want anything from you.	They become spoiled and demanding.	They don't stand up for themselves and give in to most requests.
You are overprotective and always worry that they will get hurt or sick.	They take chances and expose themselves to danger. Many become daredevils or stuntpersons.	They become overly cautious about sports and physical activities. They develop an excessive fear of injury.	They express extreme worry about your getting hurt.
You are underprotective, and ignore situations of danger.	They become overly cautious and can't easily relax and have fun.	They take chances and expose themselves to danger.	They ignore you when you or siblings are in danger—for example, if you are drunk and decide to drive.
You are dishonest.	They become obsessed with doing the right thing, sometimes to the point of moral righteousness.	They give you opportunities to take advantage of them.	They are dishonest with you and will routinely lie.
You are righteous and disdainful of others.	They will point out your faults, especially in front of others.	They will highlight their own failures, get into trouble, and become anti-social to make you feel morally superior.	They act morally superior to you.

WHY ARE MY KIDS A CONTINUAL PAIN? (continued)

What You Do to Them	When They Rebel	When They Accommodate	When They Mimic
You abuse drugs or alcohol and may become unpredictable, unreliable, and/or violent and verbally abusive.	They act hateful toward anyone on drugs or not in control. They become insensitive.	They become cautious and inhibited to avoid setting you off, or try to excessively please you.	They use drugs at an early age, and may become abusive and violent.
You are controlling and bossy.	They are stubborn and defiant.	They are excessively obedient and don't think for themselves.	They act bossy and demanding of others.

The third column shows examples of *accommodation* to your expectations. For example, if you're a perfectionist, your children may be driven to succeed and feel very anxious when performing because of their fear of failing you. As a result, either they'll fail consistently or they'll succeed but not enjoy their success. A good example is a child athlete—say, a gymnast or an ice-skater—whose life has no meaning outside of the few moments that he or she spends performing. Another example is the one-dimensional child whose life is nothing without perfect grades.

In the fourth column they behave in ways that mimic yours. In this instance they may do to you and others what you have been doing to them.

Finally, you may see combinations of these adaptations in your children. This can be confusing, but don't let it throw you. Because giving in to you makes them feel resentful, they will sometimes shift to a rebellious attitude. Then, conversely, since rebellious behavior makes them feel guilty, they may shift back to accommodation.

Remember, the reason you may feel especially provoked and disturbed by your children's *accommodation* and/or *rebellious* behavior is that it reminds you of how you adapted to your parents' problems. The most obvious example might be your anger. What's hidden beneath your anger are your own painful experiences with your parents that caused you to inhibit your personal fulfillment by *accommodating, rebelling,* and *mimicking.*

Why Are My Kids Such a Pain? Here Is the Answer

Before you became a parent, you were raised with parents and siblings who may have had some of the personality flaws I've been describing throughout this book. Most likely, you aren't aware of how these experiences have caused you to interact with your kids negatively.

Like all children, you blamed yourself for your parents' bad behavior. You automatically tried to absolve yourself by doing what they required of you no matter what the cost to you, including *mimicking* them when you became a parent, in spite of your resolve to be a better parent to your kids.

You also felt resentful about having to *accommodate* their personality flaws, and this resentment caused you to do the opposite of whatever you thought was expected of you. You hoped that they would notice this protest and reform their mode of behavior with you. Most of the time it didn't work. You also *mimicked* some of their mistakes, even though you vowed to act differently as a parent. These negative patterns have become fixed in your personality and they are the flaws that your children are growing up with. They are also precisely what are causing them to act in ways that you can't stand.

Anger, Criticisms, Rewards: It Doesn't Matter, They Never Respond

Why don't your children try to please you? Why, instead, do they continue to provoke you? If they know they'll be getting your anger, your criticism, your wrath, why make the choice to do it? It's because experiencing unpleasant or painful interactions with you is their way of showing you how they feel through behavior, instead of words. Let's examine why you find yourself so upset with their behavior.

Do Unto Others as ... You treated them unpleasantly, and now they're returning the favor. Have you been too critical, and now your child is being critical of you in return? If so, quid pro quo, and tit for tat are alive and well and, unfortunately, living in your house. Why are your kids *mimicking* you? Do they really enjoy it? No way. They not only want you to stop being critical, but they also want to see if you can manage to stay calm and unprovoked when they're criticizing you. Why? So they can learn (from you) how to survive unscathed if they are criticized again.

Okay, that sounds pretty convoluted, doesn't it? But it's similar to the way a child is attracted to a teacher or to the parent of a friend who has the same steadiness and calmness that the child is seeking from his or her parent.

Also, when they do to you what you've done to them, they're attempting to gain control over what is unpleasant for them by being the giver, instead of the receiver, of unpleasant behavior. In other words, they do the criticizing instead of being on the receiving end. And you've got to admit, the receiving end is a whole lot worse and much more unpleasant.

They Do the Opposite of What You Want   They protest against what they don't like about your behavior by *rebelling*. They'll do exactly the opposite of what you expect from them. This is their way of saying, "Mom/Dad, hey, wake up. I don't like what you're doing, and you need to listen up to that fact *and* change." So if you're cold and rejecting, you might think they'd keep their distance from you. But, surprise—instead they *rebel* be demanding your attention at all costs, no matter how bizarre and unpleasant it is for you.

Your Child Attempts to Please You ... and You Hate It   What if you've been excessively authoritarian and controlling? Attempting to please you, your child becomes submissive, obedient, and reluctant to think independently. You find yourself feeling disgusted, contemptuous, or angry at these qualities and pray that your child will show more spunk, take a little more initiative.

The problem is that it's *your behavior* that's responsible for all those traits you hate, and you don't see it.

Frustration: Your Great Advantage You catch yourself feeling angry, disgusted, disappointed with your child who demands your attention . . . excessively. Let's use that as a signal to think about what *you* may be doing to cause your child's unpleasant behavior. This will make it possible for you to change your behavior. In the past you probably became angry in an instant or completely enraged when provoked by your child's screaming, tantrums, or violence to get attention. Instead of automatically blaming your child and becoming angry, *now* simply look at the chart Why Are My Kids a Continual Pain? and locate the behavior *"They demand attention at all costs"* in the column When They Rebel.

The chart may show you that your child's behavior is *rebellion* and protest against having been rejected or ignored by you. Armed with that new knowledge, you can observe yourself to see if you were, in fact, cold and rejecting of your daughter, and realize that it actually does apply. Experiment with a more attentive, positive, and affectionate approach and see if it works. It may cause your child to be more reasonable. It may cause you to feel relieved of some guilt for having failed your child. You can take it further, too. Ask yourself, "Have I been acting this way with my child because that's how my parents were with me? How did I become so rejecting toward my own child? "Did I become this way to *accommodate* a parent who wanted to never be needed by me and so now I reject anyone who wants to be close to me? Or did I become this way to *rebel* against a parent who smothered or needed me? Or am I *mimicking* a parent who rejected me?" The charts will help you answer these questions.

Once you understand the source of your motives, you'll be able to shift your attitude. You'll realize that your child's difficulty is a response to your behavior, and therefore it can be overcome. You just have to change that behavior.

In the following example of David and his son Zach, David used the chart to solve an intractable problem with Zach, who refused to listen to anything he had to say.

▨ DAVID ▨

David was following the Golden Rule. David's father constantly criticized him. Later on, when David became a father, guess what he did. That's right: the very same thing. Zach, David's son, didn't criticize in return. He chose to do something else. He refused to listen to anything his father said. Zach's behavior was his way of protesting against all that he didn't like in his father's attitude. This frustrated David, but no matter what he did, Zach's behavior continued.

Why didn't Zach simply tell his father to quit it, to stop treating him that way? Why did he choose instead to not listen to anything David said? Some children *do* tell their parents just that. But because there's a risk that David would simply deny that he was critical, or might even get angry, it was probably easier for Zach to refuse to listen to his father rather than criticize him. Again, the reason for Zach's behavior was to get his father to stop being critical of him because it was so painful to him. But it didn't work.

Remember, getting angry with your child for criticizing you will not necessarily stop your child from criticizing you. It would be nice if it were that easy, but it isn't. Your child will probably interpret your anger as your inability to face criticism and will keep on acting this way until you demonstrate how to take their negativity in stride. ▨

Why It's So Hard to Control
Your Anger Toward Your Child

Certain people's actions or sayings just set you off, right? And chances are the quality in them that upsets you the most is the one you can't stand in yourself—but are unable to recognize. It's not too hard to figure out why, is it? It's because it's not very pleasant to be reminded of the simple fact that there are traits you possess that you don't like.

What if *you* were very hurt by *your* parent's criticism, and now you've become overly sensitive to criticism from anyone, especially your children? In your mind it's as if your parent were criticizing you all over again. And you react with the same anger you did as a child.

Now stop for a minute. If you still haven't resolved the hurt you experienced with your parents, how can you handle the same hurt you're experiencing with your children now?

Breaking the Cycle:
A Second Chance

Whatever you've tried with your kids, the rewards, punishments, and anger haven't worked, have they? So now you're ready to take the first step to gaining control over this problem. That first step is *realizing that your anger toward you child is not leading to positive change.*

The second step? Checking your family personality profiles to confirm that your parents behaved the same way with you. If they were that way with you, it might help you to feel less provoked when your child reflects that back to you. You may even feel challenged to behave better with your child than your parent did with you. You'll realize that you're part of a cycle that *can* be broken. The most important proof of your success is the improvement in your children's behavior.

Think of it this way: Your kids are giving you a second chance to deal with the problem you had with your own parents. It's actually something for which you should thank them, not yell at them, but that's not necessarily possible.

If you're provoked by their behavior with you and you deal with it in an appropriate way, it models a better way for them to deal with you. Not only that, you see how you might have responded if your parents had handled *you* correctly, and this in turn helps to lessen your self-blame.

So far we've looked at how your children may provoke you by doing to you what you did to them. But there *are* other ways they may behave in response to your behavior. Let's look at them now.

Rebellion: Do They Get Your Goat?

Remember the chart at the beginning of this chapter called "When You Can't Stand Your Kids"? It lists some of the rebellious behaviors you hate in your kids. For example, instead of responding to your criticism, they might deny your accusations and refuse to listen to any suggestions or comments you make. You might recognize this behavior as *rebellion*; you may also recognize two of the feelings it brings up—frustration and anger. If you're a perfectionist, your kids might become sloppy, careless, do poorly in school, and refuse to compete. If you're too controlling, they'll probably be defiant and stubborn. If your attitude about sex or drugs is too rigid, rebellion may turn up in the form of promiscuity or excessive drug use. If you need them to be close to you, watch as they maintain emotional distance from you, keeping their personal lives secret. Too self-centered? They'll avoid giving you credit for your accomplishments. Too moralistic about a particular subject? That'll be the exact area in which they'll get in trouble. Always give in to them? They'll push you to stand up to them. Indifferent? They'll demand attention by acting in ways that are off-the-wall. Overprotective? They'll put themselves in dangerous situations.

If you're unclear about the rebellious behavior you're observing, go to the chart called "Why Are My Kids a Continual Pain?" and locate your child's behavior. That will tell you what it is about you they're rebelling against and enable you to focus on how it developed in your own family so that you can change it.

Hate It When They Try to Please You?

You might think that you'd actually feel pleased when your kids try so hard to please you. But instead you don't. Instead, you find yourself feeling incredibly disappointed with them. What's that about? When they try to *accommodate* one of your excessive qualities, their resulting behavior may also turn out to be excessive. This is what you find so unappealing. If you're continually criticizing them, your children may accept your negative opinions of them and display a low self-opinion ("I'm no good," "I'm lazy," "I'm selfish," and so on). The result is that you may not respect them, even though they're simply trying to accommodate you!

If you're overprotective, you may find yourself feeling frustrated about having such a cautious child, a behavior that inhibits him or her from participating in, say, sports. If you're *under*protective, you'll probably be provoked when your child becomes a daredevil or puts him- or herself right in the face of unnecessary danger. Again, the most important guide is their behavior. If you change your attitude toward you children and their behavior improves, it means that you're doing right by them. Conversely, if their behavior stays the same or gets worse, you need to figure out what you need to change in yourself.

Bill improved his relationship with his two sons by comparing which of his behaviors worked and which ones didn't even come close.

▓ BILL ▓

Bill was being tested. When his nine-year-old son refused to eat his lunch at school and Bill repeatedly asked him if he ate it, his son would bring home his uneaten lunch. When Bill stopped asking about it, his son began eating his lunch at school. At the time, Bill had no clue that his son was testing him. He was seeing if Bill would stop acting worried about him (which is what he saw in Bill's intrusive daily questions) and trust him.

When Bill's seven-year-old son would say that there was something he wanted to talk about but that he was going to tell his mother about it, Bill would ask his son to talk to *him* about it. But his son would ignore Bill and instead run right over to tell his mother. When Bill stopped asking for the information, his son began confiding in him more and more. Bill used trial and error as a way of assessing different situations with his sons and then changing his behavior.

While it's sometimes possible to do what Bill did, in most instances people have a tendency to continue acting out their childhood patterns with their children until they understand the motivations for their unwanted behavior. In that case, it's helpful to compare how your children relate to your partner in contrast to how they interact with you. You might notice that one of your child's particular behaviors upsets you but doesn't provoke your partner in the least. Likewise, when your partner wonders why you're so provoked by certain situations, this should also spark some curiosity in you about the cause of your reactions. These might be very useful clues to you. They may be pointing up some heightened sensitivities you have toward your children's behavior that are actually due to experiences *you* had with your parents.

Many parents wonder if their children were simply born with the tendency to behave badly. They believe that they've done everything right by their children, but it never actually occurs to them that their children's actions may be a direct response to their own behavior. ■

Our next story is about Martin, a man who by day was a successful manager at his job but at night was a failure as a parent.

■ **MARTIN** ■

Martin was waiting to rescue anyone in distress. Martin was a successful managing partner at a consulting firm. He came in to see me at his wife's urging. She was already in therapy because of problems with their adolescent son. Martin complained that his son was casual at best about his homework and tests, constantly breaking curfews, and generally irresponsible.

When Martin would remind Mike about school deadlines, his son tended to ignore them and would barely complete his assignments, even at the last minute. Martin worried about him and approached the problem not by being strict or punitive, but by continually reminding, prodding, and attempting to help his son. But Mike's behavior didn't change. Martin's wife, Anne, took a different approach. She responded to Mike's failings by becoming critical, angry, and imposing greater restrictions. But nothing worked, and the frustrations of both parents intensified.

Martin liked his son and thought that his son liked him because he was so helpful. In fact, he said, "I want my son to like me, and as a result, I have trouble drawing the line with him and setting limits when he screws up. I worry about his problems, and I want to solve them." When I asked him if he thought Mike would behave more responsibly if he did set limits with him, he said, "I'm not really sure because it doesn't seem to make a difference when my wife cracks down."

He made the observation that he even did everything for his wife. "What do you mean?" I asked. He said, "I'm always solving her problems." Martin noted that at work, where he was the managing partner, he didn't have much fun because he was always trying to solve everyone's problems. It didn't matter if they were clients, partners, or staff—if there was a problem, Martin needed to solve it. "I worry about everyone else so much that I can't be happy unless everyone around me is happy."

Martin began realizing that his approach to Mike's difficulties was contributing to his son's continuing to act like a "flake" instead of coming around and acting successful on his own. Martin even speculated that it probably *would* be better if he stopped rescuing Mike. I asked him why, then, he *didn't* let his son manage his own affairs and experience the consequences of his actions. Martin replied that he didn't understand why he couldn't follow his own judgment about what probably would be a more effective approach. What Martin *really* didn't understand was that it was his family history that drove him to behave the way he did with his son.

Mike felt stifled and resentful over his father's hovering, worried attitude. He believed that his father's worrying about him, and his need to be liked by him, made his dad vulnerable to disappointment and hurt if

Mike acted independently. Mike was afraid of depriving his dad of the satisfaction he got from being Mike's rescuer and problem solver.

So Mike actually thought he was making his father happy by being a flake. He was *accommodating* his dad's weakness. But what about his mother? Mike resented submitting to her demanding, critical approach, and *rebelled* against it by continuing his irresponsible behavior.

Martin needed to understand the source of his behavior toward his son *and* the effect it was having on him. Once he did understand, he could use this knowledge and start changing what wasn't working. Martin had no idea that his managerial style, which was to make sure that everyone around him was happy, had its origins in his childhood family experiences. It all began for Martin with a father who worried.

And Martin's father didn't just worry; he worried compulsively. He was a hypochondriac who also thought he was dying of cancer. He was easily agitated to a state of panic and sobbing if he didn't know where everyone was at all times. He always assumed that unless he was extraordinarily vigilant, and in total control, something terrible would happen to a member of his family. At times, he limited his and his wife's social life out of his paranoid belief that people were out to get him. Eventually he got so out of control that he required hospitalization and medication.

Martin admitted that he felt sorry for his father who was disturbed. "He was a total loser, but I feel it is sacrilegious to say to so. It's brutal to not be able to say much about your father that's positive."

One of the major impacts all of this had on Martin was to make him feel exceedingly worried about upsetting his fragile father. If he wasn't vigilant and responsible, he was afraid that he'd cause his dad to have an anxiety attack. The result? Martin tried to anticipate which circumstances would disturb others, and then he tried to fix things before they got out of control. Martin developed this pattern in his childhood, but he carried it over to affect everyone in his life. Allowing his son to experience the consequences of irresponsible actions made Martin feel guilty in the same way he did with his father. For Martin, his guilt had the same intensity as it would for someone who saw that someone's about to be hit by a car but didn't warn the person.

What else caused Martin's sense of responsibility toward others? Martin had an older brother who was very jealous of Martin's athletic and academic capabilities. Even though it was irrational, Martin felt that he was responsible for making his brother feel inadequate, and this influenced him to play down his successes. He didn't want to diminish himself, but he also didn't want to hurt his brother's feelings. So, in order to *not* feel guilty about upsetting someone, Martin mastered the art of playing down his achievements.

Just as he wanted to appease his brother's jealousy and his father's excessive worry, Martin didn't want his son to flounder either. In this way, Martin's son had become the emotional stand-in for Martin's brother.

Finally, Martin's mother enters the picture, and with her came Martin's awareness that for nearly all of his life he felt sorry for her. She'd practically been imprisoned by his father's paranoia, giving up more and more of her activities as time went on. "I didn't want to introduce any additional anxiety in her life. So I never complained to her when I had problems or was worried about something.

When she asks about Mike, I always say positive things, and avoid describing the troubles he has been having."

Martin saw that he'd been *mimicking* his mother, who demonstrated that self-sacrifice was the way to deal with adversity. "It forced me to subjugate myself to the problems of others."

Martin could see how he even felt responsible in our therapy relationship. He told me that he felt obligated to be exceptionally focused during our sessions, so that I could help him make progress, which in turn would make me feel successful. "If I introduce pleasure into your life, I will feel liked. It's only when others are happy that I can be happy."

Martin was soon able to apply his new self-knowledge in his relationship with his son. Understanding the motivations for his excessive worry and responsibility toward others increasingly helped him become less managerial with his son. Mike continued to test his father by leaving his homework *un*done until the last minute. He wanted to see whether Martin would remind him about it, or tell him how to do it. But Martin avoided taking over, and he was surprised that the more he refrained, the more responsible and self-reliant Mike became.

He went so far as to create an agreement with Mike. If Mike didn't achieve a certain grade point average, he wouldn't get to use the car. When his grades *did* drop, Mike tried hard to manipulate his father to use the car for just one night, but for once Martin didn't give in. And when Mike fell just short of raising the money needed for a special school trip, Martin refused to bail him out.

The less worried Martin became, the freer Mike became to act independently. Knowing that his father would not be disappointed by his own abilities was a huge relief to Mike. ▪

Creating Family Turbulence: Siblings in Conflict

Sibling rivalries and competitions are often the major source of a parent's frustration and can be a big cause of parent-child conflicts. The sibling conflict may provoke the parent not only because he or she wants peace in the household, but also because the conflict may remind that parent of his or her own past family troubles. This could be true if:

- The parent identifies with the child who is being dominated. If this is the case, the parent may take the side of that child even when it's not justified, and excessively punish the other child
- The child who is dominated or made fun of inhibits his or her social, academic, or athletic performance; the parent may wrongly feel at fault.
- A parent who grew up in a family where high achievements were demanded will become angry and frustrated with the child who isn't performing.
- A parent who has been discouraged from doing well in life because of a competitive parent or sibling may feel guilty about being a good parent and not deal effectively with his or her children's disputes.
- A parent who as a child was jealous of a younger sibling may identify with the older child, and as a result blame or not protect the child who's being mistreated.
- A parent who had weak, ineffectual, or neglectful parents might mimic those parents and neglect the situation to the detriment of one or both of his or her children.

Let's look at an example: Laura was provoked by her daughter Carrie, who wasn't doing as well as she could due to a sibling conflict.

■ **LAURA** ■

Laura was never a burden to her mother. Laura was uncomfortable about the problems her two daughters were having as a result of a strong sibling conflict. Janice, the older daughter, enjoyed her special position as the first-born and resented the birth of her younger sister, Carrie. She picked on her little sister, and made fun of her whenever Carrie tried to stand out, perform, or do well in school. Carrie became shy and uncomfortable with compliments and attention, and she didn't do as well as her older sister. Most likely, she was inhibiting herself in order to not threaten her older sister's self-esteem.

Naturally, Laura was worried about Carrie, and not just as a concerned mother. She was also worried because her own childhood had required her to be self-reliant, independent, and strong. Laura had been raised by a cold, rejecting mother who disliked it when Laura came to her for affection, comfort, and help with her problems. So as not to be a burden to her mother, Laura became very independent and self-reliant.

Laura didn't *realize* that she felt guilty about burdening her mother and as a result didn't feel she deserved to be a better parent than her mother had been. The result? She mimicked her mother and distanced herself from her daughter Carrie, who acted the more needy of her two daughters. Laura *unconsciously* favored the older daughter, who was more like her and less needy of support, and the more she favored Janice, the more Carrie's difficulties escalated. Once Laura began to understand the motivation for her identification with her mother, she was able to become more understanding of and comforting toward Carrie. ■

About Adolescence

Adolescence is a time of turmoil. The turmoil that adolescents go through is about the conflict they're feeling over their need to reject their parents in order to become independent of them. As a result, many teenagers have a tendency to feel guilty about these strivings. These feelings of guilt become more difficult for them to come to terms with if, throughout their childhood, their parents displayed some or many of the behaviors discussed in this book.

For example, they'll experience more conflict about wanting independence if their parents have been authoritarian and controlling. In that case, you might see more passive-aggressive forms of defiance such as sneaking out at night, lying about their plans, and keeping a secret of their sexual and drug activities. If instead, you're surprised by how "good" your teenager is compared to his or her friends, it may be a sign of overcompliance with your need to be in control.

A parent who is overly moralistic or strict about sex may contribute to a rebelliously promiscuous teenager. Or if your child is excessively accommodating, you may instead notice that your child is very socially inhibited.

A possessive parent will cause adolescents to experience intensified guilt about forming close relationships both with peers and the opposite sex because they'll feel disloyal to you if they do. If you notice that they choose people who reject them, it is a means of atoning for rejecting you. On the other hand, if they rebel against your possessiveness, you'll notice an extreme emotional distancing from you.

If you've been overprotective, it will cause them to be too cautious and interfere with their need to have a sense of adventure. These kids tend to avoid competitive sports, hiking, and the like. On the other hand, they may rebel by routinely exposing themselves to danger, becoming the great daredevil and causing you to feel great anxiety.

If you're depressed and needy, they'll feel obligated to be overly attentive to you. As a result, you may notice that they have difficulty feeling happy. Rebelling is likely to take the form of indifference to the suffering in you and others.

If you're dishonest in your dealings with others, it may cause them to have difficulty doing right by people. If you notice that your child has an excessive concern with moral righteousness, it's probably a rebellion against your behavior.

In addition, you may have other qualities that can easily intensify the conflicts that adolescents experience. If you feel competitive with them, or feel threatened by their bravado, assertiveness, or sexuality, they'll become either inappropriately meek or excessively challenging. If you tend to feel easily upset by turmoil, you may become overly agitated or withdrawn in response to the changes in your children. In either case you'll be ineffective, and they'll either respond by *accommodation* and act meek to protect you, or they'll be excessively challenging as a *rebellion* against your ineffectiveness.

Exercise: Now Look at Yourself

Throughout this book, chapters with charts have not had an end-of-chapter exercise. This chapter being the last, we've included one so as to end the book with a thought-provoking exercise. If you're ready for it, read on. If you're not, skip ahead to the Afterword, and hopefully you'll come back to this last exercise in the future.

Not everyone who reads this book will become a parent, but almost everyone shares the common thread of having *had* a parent. Now is your chance to create the ideal parent, and you'll do it in the form of a job posting. It's up to you to know what you are looking for in your perfect parent, and the job posting format will help you define the qualities. A second part follows in which you look at your own parents and define those of their traits that did not meet the guidelines you set up in your job posting. To help you get started some possibilities have been sketched in for each of the categories in Parts 1 and 2. Also remember, if you were raised by a sibling or a grandparent or an aunt or uncle, those would work too.

Part 1: The Job Posting

Job: Ideal Parent (or Ideal Mother, Ideal Father)

Qualifications: [for example: Able to listen carefully without criticism. Not reluctant to stand firm ground when it is called for. Controls temper in stressful times. A strong moral sense of right and wrong.]

Special Skills: [for example: Able to demonstrate love and receive love. Sobriety. Cooking.]

Education: [for example: Advanced degrees not necessary, but able to learn new ways of parenting. Open to change.]

Part 2: The Falling Short of Your Parents

[Looking at your own parents, notice where they didn't succeed for you.]

Qualifications: [for example: My father was always critical. I couldn't even wash the car with him on Sunday morning without his criticizing the way I sprayed water from the hose. He blew up at the slightest thing, and I suspect ! c cheated customers out of money, though I never saw him do it.]

Special Skills: [for example: My father had a hard time with love. He was cold and distant. He didn't have a big problem with drinking, not every day, but when he did drink he was mean.]

Education: [for example: My father had a college degree, but I never saw him read one book or take one class that would teach him anything new.]

Keeping
the Hope Alive

WHEN YOU STARTED READING THIS book you were probably wondering if I could help you change your self-defeating behaviors. Would your long-standing struggles with your weight, your relationships, your career, or your parenting become more manageable? I didn't try to give you the usual lists you find in so many self-help books. You know the ones: "5 Ways to Instant Success," "10 Days to Lose 10 Unwanted Pounds," and on and on and on. What I have tried to do was give you a solid understanding of your problems. It was my goal to give you the tools to help you uncover what *specifically happened to you* in your family—general theories about unknown families and their vague situations weren't what I was after. Being armed with the tools described in the chapters of this book and possessed of a desire to change is, I believe, the way to lifelong success and happiness.

To achieve my intended results for you I used a three-part approach: First, I wanted to show you how your relationships with family members who had their own problems caused you to have the behaviors that you hate.

I next wanted you to understand *why* those behaviors remained hidden from your conscious awareness for so long.

Finally, I wanted you to know *how* to use the information in this book to change your life.

I hope that in accomplishing those three things I've helped change lifelong patterns and habits that were making you unhappy and were causing you to give up the hope of leading the life you really wanted to lead.

There is no way one book can solve all the problems of your life. Old problems will re-emerge; they *do* have a way of rearing their annoying heads. But now *you* have the ability to take control of them and not have it be the other way around—them taking control of you. Now when a problem comes up, you can look at your current life and find the real cause to it right then and there; it will no longer be lodged somewhere in your complicated past.

Your life is a unique journey, and every day is filled with unique challenges. Having read this book, I hope you view the challenges as constructive, not destructive, as life-affirming, not life-threatening, and as a way to *open* new doors, not slam them shut. I hope that when you see each new challenge, you also see the ways of overcoming it. And *having* overcome them, you will see broad new vistas open for you to enter and there thrive. Finally, I truly hope that this book will serve as a gateway to a more fulfilling future for you.

INDEX

A

abusive relationships, 186–191
accommodation
  about, 35–36
  accusations and patterns of,
    93–94
  combining with rebellion and
    mimicking, 50-51
  failure and, 197–201
  identifying, 52–53
  overweight and, 147
  rebellion and, 40–43
  relationships and, 37–39
  relieving guilt with, 42–43,
    57–58
  resentment and, 36, 39–40
  seeking relief with, 57–58
  understanding child's, 243–244,
    248–249
  when others act badly, 71–73
achievement. *See also* failure;
  success
  academic, 21
  case studies of failure and,
    210–226
  high standards for, 91
  inability to enjoy, 36–37, 60–62
  substitutions for, 19
adolescence, 257–258
alcoholism
  parent's, 86
  rebellion and, 51
"always be nice to others," 28–29
ambition. *See* achievement
anger
  guilt and, 98
  toward children, 232, 246–247
anorexia, 162–167

Anorexia and More (chart), 164
appeasement, 9–10, 11
assertiveness
  submissiveness vs., 28–29
  worthlessness and, 21–22
assessments
  about, 111
  charts for, 112–113, 117–120
  developing family's, 114
  for father, 116, 121–122
  for mother, 122–123
  self, 115–116
  for sibling, 123–124

B

backsliding, 129–130
behavior. *See also specific types
  of behavior*
  accommodation, 243–244,
    248–249
  compulsive eating habits,
    23–24
  conflicts in sexuality, 19–20
  coping, 70, 74
  depressive, 87
  developing self-destructive,
    56–57
  dislike of other's flawed, 64
  evaluating own, 24–25
  failures in career or academic
    goals, 21
  finding causes of, 17
  forgetting painful experiences,
    202
  free will and compulsive, 16
  genetic basis for, 60
  mimicking, 43, 242–243
  overcoming, 23

persistence of, 3, 12
placating, 30
power and patterns of self-
worth, 21–22
procrastination, 18–19
qualities undermining success,
203–208
rebellious, 243, 247–248
recognizing kid's reaction to
your, 233, 238–240, 241–245
reinforcing child's negative,
22–23
substituting fantasies for
achievements, 19
thoughts stemming from
parental, 77, 78–79
willpower to change, 5
binging and starving, 152–155
black sheep, 88
blame
blaming parents, 56
child's assuming for parents, 30
bludgeoning, 7
boasting, 207–208
brothers. See siblings

C
careers. See also failure; success
case studies relating to, 210–226
failures in, 21, 197–201
unable to enjoy success in,
36–37, 60–62
case studies
about rebellion, 58–59
anorexia, 163, 165–167
assessment of father, 116,
121–122
assessment of mother, 122–123
assessment of sibling, 123–124
binging and starving, 152–155
children reacting to parents,
249–254
combining accommodation and
rebellion, 50–51
compulsive overeating, 146,
148–152, 155–161
critical parents, 245
double trouble, 137–139

envy, 100–104
mimicking, 47–50
pathological jealousy, 98–99
rebellion against accommodation, 41–42
relationships, 38–39, 171–191
sibling rivalry, 255–256
successes and failures, 210–226
survivor guilt, 105–109, 202
thoughts about self, 77, 80
whitewashing and denial, 64–65
change
applying self-knowledge for,
130–134
backsliding and, 129–130
improving relationships, 134–135
persistence of negative
behaviors, 3, 12
willpower and, 5
charts
Anorexia and More, 164
Checking Out Your Symptoms,
117–120
Examples of Double Trouble,
140
How You Create New Moral
Rules to Live By, 74, 75–76
How Your Parents' Behavior
Can Lead to Thoughts That
Plague You, 78–79
using, 69–70
Using Sexual Fantasies to Deal
With Family Conflict, 193–194
What Happened To You When
Your Parents and Siblings
Acted Badly, 71–73, 112–113
When You Can't Stand Your
Kids, 233, 234–237
Why Am I Fat and Why Can't I
Lose Weight?, 147
Why Are My Kids a Continual
Pain?, 233, 238–240, 241
Why Can't I Fall in Love or Stay
in Love?, 170
Why Do Wealth and Success
Pass Me By?, 198–199
Checking Out Your Symptoms
(chart), 117–120

children
  accommodation by, 243–244,
    248–249
  adolescence, 257–258
  appeasing parents, 9–10, 11
  assuming blame for parents'
    flaws, 30
  conflict between siblings,
    255–256
  double trouble with parents,
    137–141
  favored by parents, 91
  forgetting painful experiences,
    202
  handling anger toward, 232,
    246–247
  idealizing parents and siblings,
    89–90
  identifying behaviors affecting
    your, 229–233
  mimicking by, 242–243
  parents' complaints about,
    229
  presuming responsibility for
    parent's behavior, 7–9
  rebellion of, 40, 243, 247–248
  recognizing behavior provoking,
    233, 238–240, 241–245
  reinforcing negative behaviors
    of, 22–23
  when parents can't stand their,
    233–237
chronic lying, 206
communicating guilt verbally, 6
competition
  fear of speaking up and,
    205–206
  success and, 208–210
complaining, 207
compulsive eating. See eating
    habits
coping, 70, 74, 75–76
critical parents, 88–89, 201, 245

D
denial
  case studies of, 64–65
  denying mistakes, 204
  of troubled family experiences,
    62–63
  whitewashing and, 63–64
depression, 87
disliking other's qualities, 64–65
double trouble, 137–141
  defined, 137
  examples of, 137–140
  with siblings, 214
drug use, 223–226

E
eating habits
  anorexia, 162–167
  binging and starving, 152–155
  case studies, 146, 148–150
  compulsive, 23–24
  emotional aspects of, 145–146,
    161–162
  family patterns affecting, 87
  guilt and, 155–156
  mimicking parent's, 45, 147,
    153–155
  pleasing parents with, 157–161
  Why Am I Fat and Why Can't I
    Lose Weight? (chart), 147
envy
  case study about, 215–219
  exercises about, 109–110
  jealousy and, 100–104
evaluating own behaviors,
    24–25
exercises
  about envy, 109–110
  about success, 227
  accessing self-knowledge, 67
  defining ideal parent, 258–260
  evaluating own behaviors,
    24–25
  listing false accusations,
    95–96
  listing impractical problems,
    32–33
  mimicking, accommodating, or
    rebelling, 52–53
  price paid for family problems,
    167–168
  uncovering hidden damage, 92

F
failure
  academic, 21
  case studies about, 210–226
  connecting family history to, 88
  limits on thinking creatively or
    independently, 203
  motivated by guilt, 202–203
  types of motivations for,
    197–200
false accusations, 93–94
families. *See also* parents; siblings
  assessing members of, 114
  competition within, 208–210
  patterns affecting eating habits,
    87
  selective memory about, 85–86
fantasies
  sexual, 192–195
  substituting for achievements,
    19
fathers. *See also* parents
  sample assessment of, 116,
    121–122
fears
  imposing on others, 104–105
  of speaking up, 205–206
fighting
  jealousy and violence, 97–99
  in order to love, 191–192
forgetting painful experiences,
    202
free will, 16

G
genetics and behavior, 60
guilt
  accommodation to relieve,
    42–43, 57–58
  childhood roots of, 3–5
  communicating verbally, 6
  defined, 10
  failure motivated by, 202–203
  internal confessions of, 94
  overprotection as source of,
    10–11
  paired with rebellion, 27, 31

  pathological jealousy and,
    97–99
  seeking relief with, 57–58
  survivor, 105–109, 202
  weight and, 155–156

H
handicapped siblings, 106–108
How You Create New Moral
    Rules to Live By (chart), 74,
    75–76
How Your Parents' Behavior Can
    Lead to Thoughts That Plague
    You (chart), 78–79

I
idealizing parents and siblings,
    89–90
ignoring others' advice, 208
improving flaws in relationships,
    46–47
inflexibility, 203–204
intimacy. *See* relationships;
    sexuality

J
jealousy and envy, 100–104

K
Kafka, Franz, 93
knife twisting, 6–7
know-it-alls, 204

L
letters to parents, 115, 126–127
listing impractical problems,
    32–33
love. *See* relationships; sexuality
loyalty, 38
lying, 206

M
manipulation, 6–7
masochism, 195
mimicking
  case studies on, 47–50
  combining with accommodation

and rebellion, 50–51
  denial as method of, 63–64
  failure and, 197–200, 201
  identifying, 52–53
  origins of, 43–47
  parent's eating habits, 45, 147,
    153–155
  understanding your child's,
    242–243
  when others act badly, 71–73
mistrust, 206
money. See also success
  anxiety about making, 219–223
  behaviors motivating failure,
    197–200
  failures in making, 21, 88,
    197–201
moral rules
  "always be nice to others,"
    28–29
  creating new, 74, 75–76
mothers. See also parents
  sample assessment of, 122–123
motivation
  for compulsive eating, 23–24
  seeking relief from self-
    defeating, 57–58

N
negative behavior. See behavior
negative outcomes from positive
    reinforcement, 91, 214
never giving credit to others, 207
nonverbal manipulation
    techniques, 6–7

O
obese family members, 87
ogre, 86–87
overweight. See weight

P
pain. See relieving pain
parents
  accommodating, 35–36, 74,
    75–76
  appeasing, 9–10, 11

arguments for blaming, 56
behaviors leading to plaguing
    thoughts, 77, 78–79
children favored by, 91
children's assumption of blame
    for flaws, 30
child's responsibility for
    happiness of, 7–9
common complaints about
    children, 229
critical, 88–89, 201, 245
dealing with adolescence,
    257–258
defining ideal, 258–260
developing assessments for,
    114
double trouble with, 137–141
eating to please, 157–161
effect when acting badly, 71–73,
    112–113
handling anger toward children,
    232, 246–247
idealizing, 89–90
identifying behaviors that affect
    child, 229–233
letters to, 115, 126–127
living through child's accom-
    plishments, 36–37
manipulative techniques of, 6–7
overprotective, 10–11
rebelling against demands of, 40
recognizing behavior provoking
    kids, 233, 238–240, 241–245
reinforcing child's negative
    behavior, 22–23
understanding child's rebellion,
    243, 247–248
when you can't stand your kids,
    233–237
whitewashing memories of,
    63–64
passivity, 104–105, 203
pathological jealousy, 97–99
perfectionism, 204–205
personal achievements. See
    failure; success
personal beliefs, 70, 74

personality profiles. *See* assessments
pets, 232
placating behavior, 30
positive reinforcement and negative outcomes, 91, 214
power
accommodation and personal, 35–36
patterns of self-worth and, 21–22
procrastination, 18–19
psychological jail. *See also* punishment
envy and, 109–110
punishment and, 93–96
punishment
mimicking and, 43–45
pathological jealousy and, 97–99
patterns of guilt and psychological, 94–95

R
rebellion
accommodation and, 40–43
case studies about, 58–59
combining with other behaviors, 50–51
defined, 40
drug use and, 223–226
failure and, 197–200, 201
identifying, 52–53
origins of, 11–12
overeating and, 147, 150–152, 155–156
paired with guilt, 27, 31
seeking relief with, 57–58
understanding child's, 243, 247–248
when others act badly, 71–73
refusing advice, 205, 208
rejection, 100
relationships. *See also* sexuality
abusive, 186–191
accommodation and, 37–38
case studies about, 38–39, 171–191

changing behaviors in, 134–135
fighting in order to love, 191–192
improving flaws in, 46–47
patterns in bad, 20
sexual fantasies and, 192–195
Using Sexual Fantasies to Deal With Family Conflict (chart), 193–194
violence in, 97–99, 100
Why Can't I Fall in Love or Stay in Love? (chart), 170
relieving pain
denying troubled experiences, 62–63
forgetting painful experiences, 202
lessening guilt with accommodation, 42–43, 57–58
mimicking for, 45–46
selective memory about family's flaws, 85–86
whitewashing and denial, 64–65
rescuing, 211–212
resentment
accommodation and, 36, 39–40
origins of, 11

S
sad sack, 87
sadism, 195
school. *See* achievement
selective memory, 85–86
self-defeating motivation. *See also* behavior
case studies of, 100–105
strategies seeking relief from, 57–58
survivor guilt and, 105–109, 202
selfishness, 28–29
self-knowledge
accessing, 65–67
applying, 130–134
finding underlying causes of behavior, 17
overcoming behaviors with, 23

personal assessments for, 111,
111, 115–116, 124–126
reviewing charts for, 70
self-worth
mimicking and, 47–50
power and patterns of, 21–22
sexuality. *See also* relationships
sexual fantasies, 192–195
underlying conflicts in, 19–20
Using Sexual Fantasies to Deal
With Family Conflict (chart),
193–194
showing off, 207–208
siblings
accommodating, 35–36, 74,
75–76
conflict between, 255–256
developing assessments for,
114
double trouble with, 214
effect when acting badly, 71–73,
112–113
handicapped, 106–108
idealizing, 89–90
sample assessment of, 123–124
Simpson, O. J., 97
sisters. *See* siblings
submissiveness
accommodation and, 35–36
guilt and, 28–29
success
behaviors motivating failure,
197–200
case studies, 210–226
competition and, 208–210
exercises about, 227
negative qualities undermining,
203–208
Why Do Wealth and Success
Pass Me By? (chart), 198–199
survivor guilt, 105–109, 202

T
thoughts about self
case studies on, 77, 80
chart on, 78–79
Trial, The (Kafka), 93

U
Using Sexual Fantasies to Deal
With Family Conflict (chart),
193–194

V
verbal manipulation techniques,
6–7
victims
abusive relationships and,
186–191
of envy, 100–104
of internal crimes, 97
justifying self-destructive
behaviors, 57
pathological jealousy and
punishment of, 97–99
survivor guilt, 105–109, 202
violence, 97–99

W
wealth. *See also* failure; success
career failures, 21, 197–201
case studies relating to, 210–226
Why Do Wealth and Success
Pass Me By? (chart), 198–199
weight
anorexia, 162–167
binging and starving, 152–155
eating to please parents,
157–161
emotional aspects of, 145–146,
161–162
family patterns affecting, 87
guilt and, 155–156
mimicking parent's overeating,
45
motivations for compulsive
eating habits, 23–24
Why Am I Fat and Why Can't I
Lose Weight? (chart), 147
What Happened to You When
Your Parents and Siblings
Acted Badly (chart), 71–73,
112–113
When You Can't Stand Your Kids
(chart), 233, 234–237

whitewashing
  denial and, 63–64
  selective memory about family's
    flaws, 85–86
Why Am I Fat and Why Can't I
  Lose Weight? (chart), 147
Why Are My Kids a Continual
  Pain? (chart), 233, 238–240,
  241

Why Can't I Fall in Love or Stay
  in Love? (chart), 170
Why Do Wealth and Success Pass
  Me By? (chart), 198–199
willpower, 5
worthlessness. *See* self-worth